Spirit of Trees

Gianna Settin

Estes Valley
Library

© 2017 Gianna Settin
Photographs by Author
All Rights Reserved.

No part of this publication may be reproduced, stored in a retrieval system, or transmitted, in any form or by any means, electronic, mechanical, photocopying, recording, or otherwise, without the written permission of the author.

First published by Dog Ear Publishing
4011 Vincennes Rd
Indianapolis, IN 46268
www.dogearpublishing.net

ISBN: 978-1-4575-5425-4

This book is printed on acid-free paper.

Printed in the United States of America

ACKNOWLEDGMENTS

The spirits of the trees, with my deepest gratitude.

Corey Bippes of Sundancer Graphics, for professional off-site graphic art and design consultation.

Bill, Jeannie, Jim, Ron, Shayna, Tony and especially Elise, for editorial comment and support.

Friends and family for listening.

All the staff of Dog Ear Publishing.

Firefighters and rescue personnel for watching over the land during the fires and floods.

Red the Wonder Dog, my devoted companion and hiking buddy, for his big heart.

BIOGRAPHY

Gianna Settin, PhD, is a psychologist and author, with extensive training and experience dealing with the challenges inherent in the human condition. She presents workshops in holistic health, and self-development, and practices a wide range of healing arts.

Strongly drawn to and connected with nature, Gianna has always sought out the wisdom of trees. Here, in a personal voice, she speaks from her heart to their spiritual significance for humans and the planet.

Gianna lives with her dog, "Red," and many trees, in the beauty of the mountains of Colorado.

CONTENTS

Preface	PREFACE ix
Chapter One	ANCIENT WALKERS 1
Chapter Two	LISTENING 9
Chapter Three	THE OLD ONES 19
Chapter Four	WAYS OF KNOWING 29
Chapter Five	DANCES WITH TREES 39
Chapter Six	SUSTAINING LIFE 49
Chapter Seven	FATE OF THE TREES 57
Chapter Eight	HAVING A VOICE 65
Chapter Nine	LEARNING 75
Chapter Ten	BEING SEEN 83
Chapter Eleven	PARALLEL LIVES 91
Chapter Twelve	LIVING TOGETHER 99
Chapter Thirteen	DARK FOREST 107
Chapter Fourteen	MUSIC OF MIGRATION ...117
Chapter Fifteen	CONCRETE PARK 127
Chapter Sixteen	SAMSARA 135
Chapter Seventeen	WINTER THOUGHTS 145
Chapter Eighteen	COMMUNION 151
Chapter Nineteen	WATER AND EARTH 163

PREFACE

Spirit of Trees is a work of the heart, of the poetry that is the nature of trees, not a work of science or philosophy. I am simply reporting upon my life with trees in a way that I hope will bring awareness of the interconnectedness of all beings. My communications with trees evolve from personal experience concerning the sacredness of all life. Spirit is intangible; yet, spiritual communication with a living being, whether human or tree, is possible for all.

It began as a tribute to the old stand forests, the Old Ones—what they have seen that they are so willing to share. It transformed almost immediately as I walked among them into what was directly spoken by the trees themselves, without words. Their witnessing of life on this planet taught me a spiritual lesson I continue to learn from them about coexistence, patience and endurance. Their value to humankind extends far beyond the known.

I can't talk about trees without talking about the entire ecosystem, including humans. Trees support life in ways that are rarely acknowledged and which most humans seem to take for granted. Trees aren't just here for the purpose of landscaping or aesthetics. They serve a multitude of functions— home to animals, birds, insects, reptiles, amphibians, fungi, ferns, flowers, even fish. Indeed, what life is a tree not involved with?

Trees to me are the poets of the plant kingdom. They speak in metaphor about the world. My perspective comes from seeing trees as key species that are harbingers of what can happen to humanity. They are endemic to practically every habitat on Earth. I was taught to respect all living beings. If wasted, this resource will soon be lost from the planet altogether— and what kind of world will that be?

The natural world is my home, more than any location, and *Spirit of Trees* is my tribute to it. A memoir that evolved over my lifetime of living with trees, and while traveling around the world, I began writing these pieces and collecting the accompanying photographs while traveling in the Pacific Northwest in 2007. The book was completed during a sojourn in the Colorado Rocky Mountains, nine years later, a fitting cycle. We humans, here for such a short stay, know little of the passing of time, compared with the trees.

A little breeze, not yet windy, slowly warming, birds in the trees the only sound. No people around to interrupt the perfection of nature. A rare day. I'm sitting with a cup of tea in the rickety green rocker on the deck of my cabin on the hill, surrounded by my old friends, the trees. I feel their spirits around me, supporting my being. They give life to the planet. We breathe together in the atmosphere and support each other in our appreciation of being upon the Earth.

Gathering herbs from the garden for my dinner, I find just the perfect spot to move a tiny Blue Spruce I found uprooted on the road. She speaks to me of not being happy where I put her. I make sure to ask her where she wants to be, and move her there, making sure she faces the same direction, and we exchange some energy. This kind of spiritual connection with the spirit of trees is an inspiration that I hope to share with others who read this book.

I have lived on the borders of many great forests. In Gila, New Mexico, I was privileged to live near the first designated wilderness in North America, the Aldo Leopold. Not the lush, wet mossy enveloping forest as is found on the Pacific West Coast. Not the majestic pine forests of the Colorado Rocky Mountains where peeling bark and needles form a rusty carpet underfoot. Yet, everywhere near a boulder outcropping is a struggling tree, drinking moisture from a rock. A sea of trees stretches as far as I can see in every direction. And their spirits call to me.

ANCIENT WALKERS

Chapter One

ANCIENT WALKERS

ON THE MUDDY ROAD to the ferry to Isle of Skye, Scotland, I pass an ancient Live Oak, surrounded by a wooden picket fence with a swinging gate. Alongside, is a green metal park bench, looking a bit out of place. A plaque states that this tree is a National Landmark. So, of course I have to stop and visit. I park, and walk through the gate, to sit for awhile.

First, I speak to the tree, saying that I am catching the ferry on holiday, having lunch with him. Perhaps that is presumptuous, for it is some time before he answers. Only one or two words come to me, so deep in timbre I can barely hear. They are more like groans. However, there are many spirits living in his ponderous branches, and they are talking non-stop. He has places on his trunk that are inhabited by whole families! At first, I can't decide if they are talking for themselves, or translating for him. The content convinces me: their talk is lighthearted and describes the trivia of daily events.

As nothing more is forthcoming from him, I take out my lunch, and start to eat my sandwich. All of a sudden, I become aware of communication from him, a kind of low current of sound, through which he tells me his troubles. He says he feels somewhat burdened by the responsibility of being a National Landmark, because so many sit on the bench near him. He thinks it would be better to not have a bench, especially not a metal one, and certainly not a fence enclosing him. He would like to be just himself, he says, alone. He gets tired, growing all the time with such heavy wide boughs. Regardless, he concludes with a feeling of a sigh, he is proud to be given this dignified role.

All this is conveyed rapidly. I am sitting here, amazed, still holding the sandwich. I stay for a long time because the rain has miraculously stopped, and the sun, rarely seen, emerges to shine upon his strong spirit. The light around him is shimmering and things shift around me a little—as if magically being transported to olden times—when entire forests covered the land. I realize this must be true, in some way, because I am traveling the Mam Ratagan, the ancient road to Glenelg, home of the 2000 year old brochs—defensive towers built by families of Picts.

I have driven at breakneck speed over a mist-topped mountain, glimpsing the peaks of the Five Sisters of Kintail, the air full of ozone and dripping with fog over the pass. Almost missing the ferry, I am the last car on the flat, wooden barge holding four vehicles. Mine only fits because it is so tiny. We set off, but wait—there is a dog, some kind of Aussie, left behind on the landing. Isn't he supposed to be onboard? As the barge pulls away, he backs off a few steps and then runs full tilt, launching himself, barely making it. The bargeman laughs and says it's his dog's only form of amusement, and that he loves the "Ahhhs" of people admiring his dog's prowess and daring. He has never missed a landing. I scratch his ears and several fleas jump off.

While on board, we get out of our vehicles, and I overhear someone talking about the Druids in Britain who have stories of walking trees. I go to the front of the barge, where a large, heavyset man with a bushy beard, is holding forth. The story goes that ancient trees once walked to clearings on the forest's edge in order to attend a gathering of the Elders. Standing in circle formation, protecting the shorter-lived beings of the land, they supposedly were seen swaying and heard groaning in unison. I raise an eyebrow at a pause, and ask, "What were they doing?" He says, in an almost incomprehensible brogue, "the greatest wisdom on Earth comes from a tree, don't you know, Lassie?" I smile up at him, nodding gleefully.

However, I am not just taking this at face value. How do such stories come about? Do they reflect facts whose original meaning has been lost over time? Could this have had a scientific explanation, such as a massive earthquake? Did the axis or the plates of the Earth move in those ancient times to cause planet-wide tremors in which everything slid, including trees? I suppose they could have "walked" that way. I think this seems reasonably sane. It is human nature to search for explanations for that which we do not understand.

Humans have undergone many a cataclysmic natural disaster and some always survive to tell the tale. Ancient peoples would've had to come up with some explanation for events that seemingly come out of nowhere. Very likely, they would have looked to the mystical or metaphysical, much in the way people do now, to explain the inexplicable. That's how the trees walked, is what I'm thinking—a combination of fact, myth, and religion.

When I get back from Scotland, I read about Druidism. It is one of the religious subgroups that still survive, that is most closely associated with trees. The Druids were a priest caste of ancient pagan Celts, and today "neo-druidism" and Wicca, and also many Native cultures, embrace the belief that everything in nature is imbued with a life force or spiritual energy. Called by many native peoples the Great Mystery, this seems to be an appropriate way to refer to that which defies understanding.

Many people have had direct contact with "spirit helpers" or guides. In contemporary religions, these are usually spiritual masters or beings incarnate. In the so-called pagan religions, animal guides are usual examples. Why not trees as spirit guides? In every case, communication with spirit takes place, either in explicit translated language, channeled information, or in silent knowledge that is passed to humans through prayer and meditation.

As an Anthropology major at Columbia University, I studied world religion in cultural perspective, and learned that many contemporary traditions around the planet today revere the tree as a spiritual being. And that it is not only myth that leads people to experience communication with trees as they do with any other living beings of the natural world. Spirit helpers and guides in various forms help humans in their journey through life and beyond.

Chapter Title

There is a feeling of sanctity about the natural world that trees embody. From ancient times, they have brought majesty into peoples' lives. I do not have to understand it. It is enough to observe and witness. I feel the spirit of trees as I feel spirit in all living beings. And I respect their presence in my life.

LISTENING

Chapter Two

LISTENING

TREES TALK. THEY TALK to each other, and they'll talk to us if we listen. The trouble is, we don't know how to listen. There was a time when people listened to all of nature. Now, having to sort through a bombardment of noise—too much, too much—our senses are overwhelmed, and we have forgotten the sounds of nature. If we listen when walking the forests, we would learn not only of trees, but also of ourselves.

We receive subtle messages from the trees, but do not recognize the language they speak. We observe the more overt signs of tree language evident in the colors, the sounds of leaves and branches, their fragrances. The more sensitive among us perceive and sense the energetic vibrational fields and auras of the trees. But few of us actually think to speak directly with them.

It might help to know that trees are way ahead of us. Like all of life in the forest, from birds to trees, they know we are coming, from our vibrations. They sense the energy and they send out feelers, like whispers, to passers-by to see if they are being acknowledged. They comment upon our passing, and some of them have a lot of fun with this. They will talk to you only if you are open to appreciating them as beings. Those who have been around a long time may be reluctant to engage with us because of what they have been through in their sometimes hundreds of years of existence: the fires, the earthquakes, but most of all, the cuttings.

As I walk in the wilderness, I touch the trees and bushes gently, and care for them in small ways, here moving an impinging branch, there noticing a budding stem. I take up a fallen Juniper berry and luxuriate in its heady scent, thanking it as I brush by. At times I tell my troubles to the trees, and they tell me theirs, as I sit on a rock under their branches. This is, for me, a spiritual experience more real than any I have had in any church.

In communicating with trees, sensitivity is essential, as is any real communication between humans. There is a mutuality in the exchange: the trees let me know their nature and I let them know mine. And what I have learned I never would have imagined! How they formulate concepts is different depending upon the species. Some are gendered, some not; some exist in collectives, some are loners; some are elders, others just starting out. Some of them don't want to talk, others are eager. They communicate through thought phrases, not words.

LISTENING

I first noticed that I was communing with trees on the last day of a meditation conference in the Catskill Mountains, an area very familiar to me. It happened while walking with some colleagues to lunch, down a stone path lined with flowering trees. Something about this triggered a memory:

I am in my early twenties. My husband and I, a young hippie couple, buy wooded land and an old chicken coop, right down the road from this conference center, in Ellenville, New York. We put everything we have into our dream of renovating the place into a home, among the trees—a dream abruptly interrupted by my husband's illness. As a result, the land was sold, and the course of my life was completely altered. Though difficult at the time, the outcome was an eventual career in psychology.

Contemplating the twists and turns of life, I brush against a small, fragrant tree—a Dogwood, I think—and it says, "You are here". At first, I think I have spoken to myself, or heard sounds similar to words—much as water running over rocks in a brook sometimes replicates the sound of the human voice. However, no, it was neither inside, nor outside of my head. I stop, and casually, because my colleagues are with me, I ask whether they heard anything. They did not.

Puzzled and intrigued, I lag behind to be alone with what happened. On impulse, looking around first to make sure no one is close by, and feeling ridiculous, I address the apparent location of the voice, the tree. I politely whisper, "Did you speak to me?" I hear, simply, "Yes." It seems to be a female voice. The conversation, if it could be called that, is like an echo, yet the words are clear enough to hear the inflection of tone and the nuance of speech coming, indisputably, from—the tree.

Some may say it is fantasy to think that communication with trees is possible, let alone that they direct specific messages to us. So, I don't tell anyone about this, being that it is the first time a tree has ever spoken to me. Talking to a tree? Yet, I am intrigued, and decide to see whether it happens again. After lunch, I arrange to pass by again. The tree doesn't say anything. I figure that my experience is an anomaly based upon fatigue or maybe stimulated by all the meditating I am doing at the conference, and forget all about it.

Back home in Maine, I am in the garden, admiring the baby vegetables in the raised beds, when I become aware of receiving communications from the plants all around me. Finally, it dawns upon me that I have been talking with the plants all along! I rescue them from harm, touch them to help move away an insect or flick mud off a leaf, admire their every nuance, tell them of their beauty. I ask them what is wrong when they are ailing, reassure them, and send them special energy. I even sing to them. It has always been this way, no matter where I am, indoors, outdoors, at a friend's house, in a department store. I just have not given importance to the fact that plants and I have a special relationship. They thrive, and I thrive too, in their presence!

Once I acknowledge to myself that this phenomenon is more than merely "good gardening", I name my private nursery Beech Ridge Botanicals, and expand my interest in plant communication. The information I receive at first is subtle, like a slight breeze that passes almost un-noticed, yet it is undeniably a form of communication. Once I trust the process, the experience becomes tangible and overt.

Being a scientist, I explore further. I think it is possible that conscious contact with spirit, developed through meditation and prayer, has increased my sensitivity and made me more aware of the kind of gentle knowingness that comes from plants.

Some types, I seem to have a special affinity for, such as Medieval herbs. The big medicinal herbs, like Black Cohosh and Comfrey, seem to talk the most freely with me, waving in the breeze. I have not yet moved on to trees, though. I go along like this all summer, still not telling anyone about it. My every contact with the plants seems to have an enhanced meaning. I am discovering a spiritual dimension to the process of working with plants, and it is amazing.

In the autumn, I begin to walk differently through the woods outside the gardens, more open to the trees. The Spruce, Pine, Maple, Oak, Birch and Beech, stretching far down to the lake in a swath of green, gold, brown, and yellow, come alive for me in a new way. At first I am very skeptical of the thought forms that come into my mind from trees, because they are strikingly different from the energetic contact I am used to with garden plants, vegetables, herbs, and bushes. When I consider why this is, meaning no offense to annuals and small perennials, I think it has something to do with the longevity factor. Compared with garden plants, who are often preoccupied with themselves, trees take the long view.

Alert to these experiences, I begin to experiment on hikes in the woods and forests. Ranging further afield, I find that I am listening more acutely with all my senses, more aware of my surroundings. Often, as in my first time with the Dogwood in the Catskills, a certain amount of openness is required in order to hear.

Trees are the poets of the plant kingdom. They speak in metaphor about the world. However, when they give advice, they are direct. The old ones have a very dry sense of humor. They have nothing personal to say unless they trust you, a desirable trait in humans too. I can describe talking with trees by comparing it with animal communication. It is similar, in that trees and animals both pick up on unconscious thoughts, or feeling states. They "speak" assuming that they are being heard. Once the opening occurs, they form their communications directly in response to human questions. Trees are slower in their translation than most animals, and briefer. I think perhaps they have more layers of skin, so to speak, to go through.

I have tried to find a scientific explanation for how trees and humans interact. The science of molecular physics and biochemistry has much to offer in the way of theory, yet I remain at a loss for a completely logical explanation. That is because communicating with trees is not based upon logic. It's like hearing an echo—more than an intuition, less than a voice—of a meaning followed by words. The thing is, it comes into awareness as language!

When a tree speaks, the meaning enters my consciousness through some kind of translation process. Neither the tree nor I are actively translating—it just happens. Therefore, I conclude that there a spiritual dimension to the energy passing back and forth that is involved with this feat. It is a very pleasant kind of mind melding, quasi-spiritual interaction.

As a native English speaker and dreamer, my translation comes in English; if I were Spanish, it would be in that language. I know this because I have spoken to people in different countries who report conversations with trees. It is said that when you dream in a language, then you have become a native speaker of that language. This may change over a lifetime. I have had that experience after living and working in France for a few years. But now I dream again in idiomatic English. It's like this, that the language of trees is received.

It is all so thought provoking and amazing, that I decide to spend as much time as I can, talking with as many different species of tree as I can. Traveling around the United States to talk with them, and encountering them on travels around the world, I find an astonishing diversity. And it seems as though everyone, no matter from what walk of life, has a personal story to tell when finding out about my interest in communing with trees. Other peoples' experiences, as well as my own, have been consistent. Listening to the trees, and to humans alike, makes clear the immense complexity of living beings—and how little we really know.

THE OLD ONES

Chapter Three

THE OLD ONES

 DRIVING UP THE PACIFIC Coast Highway of the United States, I pass through groves of the Old Ones. These giants draw me off the road, time after time, into their enveloping cloak of deep healing vibration. A profound peace—the silence of the ages. Stopping often, taking my time to wander slowly through groves right off the road, I confirm what I have suspected: each tree species has a distinctly different presence.

For example, the big Pines are definitely loners. Whether males or females of their species in gender, they have a more masculine presence standing alone. And then, there are the individual personalities too. That's true for us all. Like the iris of the human eye, each one different enough so that not one among millions of humans are the same. I wonder if trees are as uniquely differentiated. Why wouldn't they be? They are biological beings, like humans.

On the other hand, Spruce speak individually and identify themselves as male or female. Their root system, unlike the pines, is shallow, so that they are more likely to topple unless rooted firmly into rock and clay. One gigantic tree tells me "I metastasize into others like me." That was the concept she used, in language that frightens humans but which, for a tree, means expansion and survival!

First, I visit the Coastal Redwoods (also called Sequoias) in Northern California—old growth forests with trees over 200 years old. Redwood roots intertwine and graft onto one another, helping to hold each other up, since their roots grow only a few feet down into the soil. In some cases up to 1700 species of plants and animals may depend upon one tree during its life span.

The Redwoods seem to have a group consciousness in which the collective "We" is more important than the individual. They talk with each other. Speaking for the group, one says, "Many, many times ago we witnessed a great flood. We will go on. We will survive." Attesting to this bold statement of endurance, my attention is caught, while driving on later that day, by tsunami warning signs along the highway.

In the Humboldt Redwoods State Park in California, a temperate coniferous forest on the North American continent, I find the largest accumulation of plant mass ever recorded on Earth, according to the Humboldt Interpretive Association. Can you imagine a place where there is a biomass seven times as great as is found in a tropical rainforest? Many have been through fires in their long lifetimes and continue to live and create their own microclimates. I photograph myself next to the Dyerville Giant, a Redwood taller than Niagara Falls, who stood proudly there for 1600 years. Very few champions like him remain on the continent. When he fell in 1991, they say the Earth shook.

Further up the coast, I take a detour to drive up to Mount St. Helen's in Washington state, site of the largest recent (1980) volcanic eruption on the West Coast of the United States. I pay my respects, rejoice in the new growth— indeed, it is more like a whole new forest! Fresh, strong, from the ashes. Walking on a short path close to dusk, I talk with a beautiful Spruce, by the name of Machtepelaga. She has a lot to say. I scribble furiously in my notebook, "As we hold the rhythm, we bring in newness, because the rhythm is creation. It is the first step of reconnection. You are the broadcast of the rhythm of the Earth". I think, but no one hears her anymore... and it is right then that I realize she is telling me to somehow get out the word, literally, to broadcast something important for humans to hear.

The next day, I'm looking forward to taking a break from driving at Lake Quinault. On the way to lodgings, on North Shore Road, I drive past a sign indicating, simply, "Western Red Cedar". I am tired from so much driving, and operating on some level of awareness that I am not conscious of. An intuition tells me to stop here. It is raining, of course. Regardless, I park and start up the path above the sign, feeling that I must visit, now. As I make my way through the rainforest, I lose the trail. Fairy light filters through the canopy. It is soggy and slippery under dripping moss and I am soon covered in dirt.

While wondering what to do next, a small white dog appears. Clean and cheerful, she has not one drop of mud on her, nor collar of any kind. She informs me that her name is Jenny. Then she trots slightly ahead and, in classic spirit form, looks back as if to beckon me onward. "Is she real?" my sleep-deprived brain asks. She is—and keeps pace with me, never leaving my side as I slip up and down slick, gnarly embankments, until I regain the path.

Finally, we come to small sign announcing that this is the Old One. I look around, not seeing a tree, until I recognize that he is so massive that I cannot take him in at a glance. I must turn round to encompass his 761 inches of girth. I am standing upon scraggly roots of ancient origin and it is hard to tell if he is even alive, so still is he. His 159 feet support massive limbs, and mossy roots trail off in all directions, to far off places. Several vacant areas lie between these, and I am puzzled. Then I see that what I took to be roots, are each a giant fallen part of him—misshapen, broken, covered with scars and other vestiges of his long history on Earth. He seems to be a remnant of some past civilization. Some might almost pass him by without seeing him.

As I always do, I ask permission to place my hands on him. I receive the usual signal, a minor feeling of dislocation and a kind of spinning vortex of light behind my eyes, followed by a strong sense of my hands melding with his outer layer. Unable to move them away, a bond establishes between us. The most ancient of his clan, he speaks to me immediately when I ask his name. It is Cooahwhey. I tell him that I am honored to be in his presence, to be included in the mystery of the ages.

A loving energy emanates from his tangled form. "Blessings from Cooahwhey," he says, and tears start into my eyes. His visitors are weary travelers like myself, and eager tourists, impatient children, reluctant dogs—all discover him along their path. His magnificence is not outwardly manifested; hardly could he be called beautiful. But his interior life is a miracle.

How old is he? No one knows. So I decide to simply ask him. He says, slowly, each word separated by a pause, and with a tinge of humor, "I am very old." With my hands upon him, I listen. He tells me a beautiful song, in his language. I do not try to understand it, only to remember. Its melody is simple and haunting. He is passing to me something of his spirit that I cannot fathom in words, but in which I feel a deep resonance. It's like talking to God.

This communication stays exactly in my mind. I do not have a good memory for some things, yet this song has entered my subconscious in another language that I seem to know. It is as if the people who inhabited this forest long ago have given it to me in their language, unchanged.

Time passes. I don't know how long I stand there. Gradually, I get moving and skid down the hill. Along the trail, I am disoriented by the mystery of what has happened and pay no attention to where I am going. All at once, there is Jenny, waiting at a bend. She trots ahead of me, sits at the bottom of the trail, and waits for me to take her across the road to a house. The owner tells me that she is never gone all day like this. All day? There were many people walking that trail and crossing that road, I think to myself. Did she lead me to Cooahwhey and wait to make sure I got back safely?

Settled in my lodgings, the song of Cooahwhey in the back of my awareness, I lie down for a minute and am entering a long passage into the center of a mountain. At the end is an oval room filled with sleeping bears, big guys, maybe a dozen of them. They are curled tight on their sides, golden colored muzzles covered here and there with huge black paws. I thread myself through them, being careful not to awaken them, to the back of the cave, where there is a waterfall. On a ledge in back of the waterfall is a huge glowing aquamarine. I slip in between the water and the stone, touch it, and then am back in my room, no longer tired.

My first thought is, "Let sleeping bears lie." I know at the time what that means in my past experience. Here, though, the bears are wisdom bears—for bears are teachers. The feeling is of something waiting to be awakened at the end of a long sleep. Maybe it is I who am hibernating, dormant? And when I awaken, on the other side of the water, I will find something beautiful. I realize that in having navigated my way safely through the cave, without awakening them, I have been already transformed.

The next day, leaving the rain forest, I drive past the sign on the road, pointing uphill. I hope the path stays as it is, obscured, almost inaccessible. And that each person guided to receive Cooahwhey's message, learns that words are not necessary. Spirit comes at the exact right time and way it needs to.

It will be many years before I know the full meaning of his song.

WAYS OF KNOWING

Chapter Four

WAYS OF KNOWING

 WHAT ARE THE WAYS OF knowing that allow humans to communicate with trees, and for them to transmit information to us? The tree does not have a brain as we know it. Rather, it has a core, a place where biological and physiological functioning converges. Trees have their own particular energetic molecular structure that enables them to respond to information in a form that does not rely upon logical human brain processes. In other words, interspecies connections may be facilitated by sensory input, rather than by the complex information processing system of the human brain.

There is an energetic pathway located at the crown of the head that, in the ancient language of Sanskrit, is called a chakra. Meaning "whirling vortex of light," it is thought to be a pathway for spiritual awareness to enter. It is perceived by many as a golden glow around the head, a kind of halo. The crown of the head is also where the corpus callosum—the opening between the left and right hemispheres of the brain—is located. I like to think of this as an opening into more finely tuned knowledge, or intuition.

Children seem to initially possess ways of knowing that rely upon a sensory orientation to the world, including a kind of sixth sense. During the acculturation process, with exposure to social and mental conditioning that relies so heavily upon logical abilities, many adults end up minimizing the importance of intuition. Yet, the ability to rely upon this inner knowing is always there, waiting to emerge. It merely requires a willingness to bypass the usual uses of the brain, and a reopening of all the senses, including the sixth.

I think of the pineal gland, when a discussion of that indefinable sixth sense comes up. A part of the endocrine system, the pineal is located near a major language center of the brain and behind the forehead. It is sometimes referred to as the "third eye" because it receives waveforms of vibrational energy that heighten sensitivity and perception. According to some, it can be fine-tuned to receive and transmit intuitive information. This may stimulate the reception of such language as is emitted from non-human organisms.

What does this have to do with trees? Well, a tree encounters the auras or energy fields of the many beings to which it is exposed. It responds to stimuli, stores information. When I am standing in the energy field emitted by a tree, I feel it. The tree is also affected by mine, and a positive vibration can foster growth. A study conducted with plants in a university greenhouse, demonstrates that the plants exposed to peaceful, consonant music show better growth; in another study, using data captured on video, seedlings noticeably recoil when approached with scissors. This is why, when I walk toward a tree with clippers to prune it, I do so with conscious intent to do no harm. I talk to the tree, and handle it with care, as I do with all living beings.

As trees respond to humans, so humans respond to trees. People say that they usually experience a sense of invigoration around trees. Imagine thousands of trees, vibrating along with us while we stroll along a wooded path. Japanese researchers found a significant increase in natural immunity in men who spent merely a few hours in a forest over a space of two days. Their immune system was boosted significantly, as measured by blood samples, and the effect lasted for over a month, reportedly prompting some companies to add "forest therapy" to their health plans. Clearly, something is happening here of deeper significance than just a nice walk in the forest.

The physical functioning of the human body is affected by the vibrational frequencies emitted by all organisms. There is an energy field, or vector, surrounding the exchange that occurs when the auras of living beings touch. It is not fixed, it ebbs and flows like the tides and rolls in and around us like the swells of ocean waves. I feel a heart connection with a tree, and that is the waveform of energy I have come to associate with particular physical sensation, similar to deep affection, compassion, even love. There are many kinds of love. Trees have a deep core called heartwood. Does the tree know feelings? Perhaps not as we define them.

A tree may not "feel" or "think" as we define it, but it lives and breathes and responds to the natural frequency pulsation of the planet, as do all living beings. This frequency of the Earth's electromagnetic field is referred to as The Schumann Resonance Vibration. When beings are in entrainment with each other, meaning that their energy intersects and harmonizes according to this pulsation, a kind of harmonic convergence is created. The possibility of applying this theory of resonance and entrainment, to the tree-human interface, is interesting.

The core of a tree knows and is conscious of something. Research from the HeartMath Institute suggests that, "...the heart's big energetic and magnetic field functions as a kind of subtle intercommunication between individuals. This is often felt as attraction or repulsion, but it is more than that. Individuals in this state become more aware of the information encoded in the heart fields of those around them" (*Reiki: The Mystery Teachings*, Kidwell and Settin, 2012, p43). This psycho-physiological coherence increases sensitivity, empathy, intuition and even nonverbal communication between individuals and other living beings. All life on the planet is affected by this principle. It is conceivable that the pulsations and rhythms of different species might exchange converging patterns with each other, resulting in communication that is more than a merely biochemical way of knowing.

Meditation and prayer is one of the ways that people, across all cultures, access intuition. This indefinable experience comes about by allowing the usual ways of knowing—reasoning, feeling, perceiving—to become secondary to a physiological state of deep relaxation. Subtle energies can be experienced with all the senses, this way. Described variously as bringing peace, calm, wellbeing, or simply—

being—this experience is very pleasant. One of the ways I meditate outdoors is to shift awareness outside of myself. In this way, I can meditate in nature upon a particular tree, or rock, or on water. My perspective is immediately altered by being connected to something greater then myself.

At my cabin in Colorado, there is a meditation bench, an old church pew from an antique store in New York, that I have brought with me wherever I move. Tucked under some Ponderosa Pines on a path leading down to the creek. I sit there when I feel like it, and take in nature with all my senses. I hear sound of the water, smell the sap of the trees and of the native wildflowers and bushes blooming along the path in the spring and summer: Boulder Raspberry, Cinquefoil, Currents, Potentilla, Bearberry. Especially fragrant is crushed Artemesia, a wonderful plant for clearing energy. The bench faces East. If I can get out of bed early enough to see the sky lighten as the sun filters through the trees, and witness the miracle of awakening of life, it sets me right on my path for the whole rest of the day.

Hiking out back of the cabin, into the wilderness, there is a clearing in a field that is just open enough to have sun, even in the winter. Mindful of ticks, I sit on a log and shift my attention to the enormous rock face in front of me. Named Grandfather by a dear hiking friend, he is definitely old. Depending on the light, his face is either solemn and stern, or slightly bemused and benevolent. I think he sees a lot out there! Once I climbed all the way up onto his massive head to see what he sees. The trees just go on nonstop to the mountains beyond, seemingly forever. I have hiked many miles there with my old dog, Red, for years. Rarely do we see a person.

My strongest way of knowing, my sixth sense—intuition—is enhanced remarkably by meditation in nature with trees. Sitting, I am mindful of movement, both mine and all of the beings around me, and notice things more acutely. My brain is not "thinking". Everything is clearer. It feels as though I am vibrating as one with the pulse of the Earth. The best way for me to access this is in a walking meditation. Meditation in motion allows me freedom. It doesn't have to be walking, it can be hiking, though the slower I go, the more I perceive, and the more mindful I am of the beauty. It combines all the ways of knowing, including movement, into one.

With each step I take in the forest, my intuitive sixth sense seems to arise from, and at the same time bind together, the experience. I hear the sounds of the tree's leaves, see the motion of the branches, taste the fruits, smell the scent of the bark, feel the wind sighing through the branches. And the trees seem to be more alive too. It's an unparalleled spiritual experience.

This traditional Navajo song reminds me, as I experience the woods and forests, what it feels like to walk with the spirits of trees:

> *"In beauty may I walk.*
> *All day long may I walk.*
> *Through the returning seasons may I walk.*
>
> *"Beautifully will I possess again.*
> *Beautiful birds....*
> *Beautiful joyful birds...*
>
> *"On the trail marked with pollen may I walk.*
> *With grasshoppers about my feet may I walk.*
> *With dew about my feet may I walk.*

"With beauty before me, behind me, above me,
all around me may I walk.
In old age wandering on a trail of beauty
lively, may I walk.

"It is finished in beauty.
It is finished in beauty."

DANCES WITH TREES

Chapter Five

DANCES WITH TREES

"TALK WITH US, DANCE with us," are the words given to me by a circle of Redwoods in Northern California. I am taken aback. I have not been trying to communicate. I am just meditating on a log, once a tree, appreciating their magnificence. Do they recognize me? Do they know I am a dancer? Or do they feel my feminine gender, some energy that called to them.

These Redwood giants seem to have a feminine aspect to their being. Perhaps it is that they reach out to me as a group, as would a family of women sensing the presence of one of them in need. Their roots spread from the center outward, to create new seedlings. This family energy connects me to the Earth, to some deep nurturance of what is called, for good reason, "mother" Earth. It feels as though they bend inward, looking down, to embrace me. This impression is strongly conveyed, intuitively. I must seem so young and a bit lost at the moment. It is true. They invite me to join them in more than merely physical movement—they ask me to join with them in spirit via the creative act of dancing.

In contrast, teaching a Healing Dance workshop in France, I am in a gymnasium with metal poles holding up the ceiling, instead of trees holding up the sky. Too cold and rainy to be out, we are in inside for two days. At least the floor is wood! Finally able to go outside, we practice joyfully merging healing energy by dancing with an old grand Cedar of Lebanon, who is happy to have us circling and celebrating with him. Even straight-laced students, who have to be coaxed to dance with a tree in full view of onlookers, lose themselves in the experience of touching the tree trunk, having their feet on the ground above the roots.

There has always been a ritual or ceremony in the history of all people, that honors the tree. Whether dancing around the Maypole or circling an ancient Live Oak in Dances of Universal Peace, what matters is the meaning and spiritual essence of the celebration. Trees represent renewal of life. People come together to dance, not just for sake of dancing, but to solidify their ties and renew their spiritual vows to themselves, to their community, and to the planetary spirit.

Here, Two Crow shares his experience, from a Native American perspective, about the spiritual meaning of the tree, not only for ceremonial ritual, but for the wisdom lesson that comes when a tree decides to speak:

"After many years of participation in Sun Dance, first as a Dancer and then as a Helper, my Sun Dance Intercessor selected me to lead a team to capture the tree. This follows an old tradition where a group of warriors selected and then counted coup on a tree (sometimes the tree was preselected by the Intercessor and cared for throughout the year). I selected three other Helpers who had many years of experience at Sun Dance and whom I had danced with and/or helped to complete their commitment. While the cottonwood is typically the tree used for the center or medicine pole, at the location we held our ceremony we used an alder tree.

"I lead a group to have a tree select us. We wandered for more that an hour after one had called to me, "I want to go dance with you, please take me." The fork on this one seemed to be too close to the ground so I listened to the group conscious and we took more than an hour looking for a higher fork. When I came back around the original tree, she spoke again to me, "Look, how important is size anyway...look at you! Why you are just a bit over 5 feet tall yourself and yet a seasoned dancer and helper. Please take me to dance one last time with you...after all while my spirit is eternal my physical entity is ephemeral. I would be so honored to spend my last breaths sharing medicine at the ceremony." The logic and sincerity overwhelmed me... She is the one for this year's Medicine Pole. When we had carefully chopped Her down, we saw that Her core was indeed already dead. That year's ceremony was blessed with moderate weather, strong committed dancers and was a sweet ceremony."

Trees also have an integral role in the system of shamanic healing. A shaman is often said to gain entry to other worlds or dimensions, energetically speaking, by entering under the roots of an immense tree. By connecting with the spirit of a tree, the "shadow self" can be brought up the surface. To restore wholeness, parts of the spirit that may have become separated from the self, are retrieved so that the person's spiritual, emotional and physical aspects can re-integrate. As in many Native American cultural traditions, this process is conducted by trained medicine persons, according to specific rituals.

The use of the tree as a metaphor for discovering the source of illness, is lost to Western medicine. However, the principle that the root of disease or malaise needs to be uncovered, in order to release impediments to health, is common to all medical approaches. By restoring molecular flow to systems that are blocked or impaired, all parts of any living being experience improved health or restored function. The basic mechanics of healing in both Western and Eastern medicine systems, including the concept of mind-body-spirit interface, is agreed upon, though the vocabulary and treatment approaches are usually quite different.

For a long time, I have practiced and have taught Reiki, a Japanese energetic approach to wellness, and combine it with dance as a healing modality. The vibrational frequency of Reiki—a subset of Universal Chi—is a highly sensitive harmonizing energy that entrains with the energy of the recipient, bringing it back into balance. All living beings are receptive to Reiki, and trees especially so. In fact, they resonate with its frequency so well that it almost seems as if they are already attuned to it!

Reiki is related in its philosophy to the Dao, and also somewhat to Shintoism. Known as the "way of the gods," the concept is that a sacred essence called "kami", or spiritual aspect, is found in all living beings: people, animals, mountains, and trees. As I conceive of it, Reiki with trees has a similar spiritual essence, in which nature and the elements act as powerful adjuncts to healing.

I have often healed faster from imbalances in my system, by combining Reiki and dance with contact with trees. The combined flow of merging energies of movement appears to potentiate the power and effectiveness of the experience. Chi energizes the molecules in the cells of every living being. When my aura intersects with a tree's aura, the chi intensifies. Movement facilitates the flow of chi. And it is not only physical—it is my entire multilayered system that is stimulated by chi. It's a very subtle dance of energy. I am affected in a way that does not happen when I am dancing alone or with a group of people.

Trees serve as guides for human healing. Dancing with trees helps to bring me into synchrony with my body. Seeing trees dance in the wind reminds me that that the kinesthetics of trees are really not that different from those of humans. Through imitation of form—for example, bending in a high wind instead of standing rigidly against it—my perception of my body position is mediated by receptors in muscles, tendons and joints. By mirroring the movements of trees, new patterns emerge and positive changes in functioning occur.

When the Redwoods in California asked me to dance, I really didn't now what they meant, though I intuited it. Now I understand. It was an invitation to communicate that would be mutually beneficial. Exchanging energy in combination with movement would be something with which they are familiar, since they are constantly moving in nature with the elements.

For me, dancing with trees is an interactive form of meditation and prayer, a central part of my Higher Self that connects me to nature. People who dance with trees are drawn to do this for their own spiritual reasons—for the big heart connection with the spirit of the trees themselves.

The tree represents something central to my being. I cannot explain why, I only know that I feel completely at one with spirit when I connect in this way with trees. In no other way do I as strongly realize my relationship to the Earth. What a gift, to be grounded and transported at the same time, to be deeply rooted and also expanded into the sky. I dance with the trees to celebrate together with them the privilege of being alive on this beautiful planet.

SUSTAINING LIFE

Chapter Six

SUSTAINING LIFE

 IT'S WINDY AND I FIND shelter under a big Fir, diameter four feet, who lives inside a protected area of Colorado wilderness. No ax falls in this deep, quiet forest in the canyon along the seasonal stream. No person bumbles through the tangled berries and Cottonwood. Only the fox, the deer trimming the edibles away, and the bear.

Shivering a little, in this late autumn, I crouch and curl into a shallow hollow in the Fir's friendly trunk, to conserve warmth. On the already rock hard ground, crumbling granite crunches beneath me, while still colorful Aspen leaves blow around my head in swirls. The Fir's soft fallen needles carpet the ground in a thick coverlet, warming us just enough. He doesn't need much cover. Trees know what is good for them. I compare notes with myself about just how much I know about survival—not as much he does, I imagine.

This Fir hardly ever speaks. I sit here often. I ask him what he thinks about these times, to make conversation. There's no answer, just his companionable presence. Once he did indicate that he enjoys the critters digging around his topsoil roots, aerating and fertilizing him. He's a quiet friend who I love to visit.

The first snow will be early this year in the Glen. No surprise there; the squirrels have been at it for a month, stripping pinecones and dropping them explosively from the heights onto the deck of my cabin. I walk up the hill above the cabin almost every day to where the ax did fall. A field of stumps remains here a century later. I see the old Cedar, who loses more branches each year to hunters building a shelter or someone wanting a twisted post for a porch. Or, more likely, to a hiker wanting wood for a fire. The passerby sees an old dead tree. Not so—the trunk remains alive. This Cedar slowly, very slowly, over the time of one human generation, sends forth new growth from underground. Now there is a circle of young Cedars surrounding—and the center lives on.

How some survive is a mystery to me, like the Creosote bushes along the path to the outhouse. While not full-fledged trees, they have characteristics similar to Cedar, yet I don't make the connection. I ask them if they would mind being pushed back out of the way, so they don't snag me as I pass by headlamp at night. Had I more carefully followed their hesitant response, in which it seemed as if they were looking at each other and wondering how to say no, I would not have proceeded. Bushes are usually not as emphatic and clear, as trees.

Even gently guiding them back, while trimming off little pieces, they break off uncontrollably. The bark strips back and exposes living parts, and the roots, barely anchored in friable soil, pull loose. I stop what I am doing immediately. Trying to make amends, I explain, and place some sage around them, but one bush will not rebound from the damage. The best kinds of amends are living amends; I won't make this mistake again.

Inside, in the woodstove, the broken limbs burn hot in the fire. Moses and the burning bush, spontaneously combusting in the 140 degree heat of the Sinai Desert, comes to mind. At least they were put to some good use, I say to the dog lying in his customary place by the fire. I'm just trying to make myself feel better, but it doesn't work.

When I move out of New York City, after I finish graduate school, I apply for jobs in Maine. The homesteaders Helen and Scott Nearing are my role models. Only later do I find out that I can't possibly afford to live like they did, because I have to hold down a full time job. Still, it planted a seed for future generations looking toward sustainability.

I end up in Maine, and look forward to heating with wood instead of electricity. The house I buy has a ten acre hardwood lot, which by my calculations, will supply firewood forever if it is well managed. I feel virtuous heating with wood instead of with electricity. I love everything about wood: stacking it, smelling its sweet and pungent aroma, and the challenge of getting a nice mixture of hard and softwood to make the best fire I can kindle in my trusty Vermont Castings stove. Staring into the fire, time hypnotically slows, and worries unwind from my busy mind. The whole process feels so satisfying in its self-sufficiency.

The fragrance of wood brings back memories of my mother's black potbelly stove in the Berkshire Mountains, and how, for a special visitor, she would throw a stick of apple wood into the firebox. I recall the secure feeling of wrapping myself up in a blanket in the rocker, close enough to the woodstove feel the radiance and just far enough away, so as not to get burned.

After several years of cutting, hauling and splitting wood from my own woodlot, I grow weary of getting up in the middle of subzero nights to throw in more wood. But, the main reason I back off is that I wake up to the fact that not only am I participating in some serious air pollution, even though I am leaving a smaller footprint, I am also using up trees! Living beings like myself. Though seeming dead for all intents, the wood is living still. Once the penny drops on that one, I borrow money and put in an efficient, high-end Italian furnace. Is this a better solution? Fossil fuels don't grow back at all! This isn't like the old days anymore.

Choices have to be made about what is important to use trees for, and what is not. I find that I have to re-evaluate my energy usage priorities every several years. Yet, I keep falling back on wood, and when I move to the mountains in Colorado, I think, "Here we go again." My little cabin in the mountains is built on a steep granite hill. It has a fabulous wood stove and an enormous old stone fireplace from basement to attic. Built in the 1930's, wood and kerosene were the only sources of heat, and water was levered up in a rigged bucket from the creek below.

At this point, I can no longer delude myself into thinking that I am doing something good for the environment by burning wood—or pellets, gas, propane, and certainly not coal. To do so either uses up a resource that takes countless years to grow back, or depletes it forever. There are ways to harness energy that don't deplete resources. My ideal solution is to live off the grid. However, when I find out the cost of installing the machinery and maintaining it to use "free" sources of heat, such as solar or wind power, I cannot afford it. And I cannot in all conscience afford not to . . .

Today, resting silently on my haunches under the big Fir, I watch a couple of elk pick their way along the side of the frozen stream. They slice open the ice with their hooves in order to drink the pure, cold water. Their coats are warm. I wish my life could be that straightforward, living according to the rhythms of Nature, where trees are central to sustaining the spirit of their lives. The idea of living in the forest calls out something in me that seems so familiar. Thankfully, I look into the sky and see tall trees towering above me instead of cell phone towers, and for the simplicity that is so out of step with the ways of the world outside.

FATE OF THE TREES

Chapter Seven

FATE OF THE TREES

AN INTERMINABLE HIGHway runs through the plains of America, and I am on it, heading for the Pacific Northwest Coast. I long for trees. Sometimes I see one or two of them in a field, alone, marking a boundary or locating a boulder that could break a tractor axle. A crow perches on the top of a single tree, cawing into the sky. It is a bleak and unforgiving landscape, some of it not even planted with crops anymore, and the dust blows away the soil.

I have plenty of time, driving across the plains, to reflect upon the places where seas of trees still exist, and start to see a pattern. It is in the National Forests and Parks, and Wilderness areas of America, where trees are protected these days, not the open ranges of the past. However, even lands set aside from exploitation, including irreplaceable ancient groves of the Old Ones, are now being threatened.

Eventually reaching Washington, where there are still many trees—at least for now—a logging truck turns out in front of me. Backing off a safe distance, and opening my windows to inhale the scent of Pines, I hear "whomp, whomp, whomp." Looking out to discover the source of the noise, I see a completely denuded mountain. Multi-national logging conglomerates are helicoptering onto the crests of mountains and logging off the tops. Erosion is an intended consequence, undermining the root systems of trees below on the mountain, conveniently toppling them all, so that they are easier to harvest.

Logging has always been a big part of the American economy, especially in rural areas. I used to live near Bangor, Maine, a famous logging town. There, the tree industry is still in full swing, although not "the way life used to be"—a Maine motto. The last log drive took place in 1976, there on the Penobscot River. In the old days, trees were skidded out of the forests by oxen to sawmills located on the waterways. Then men standing on the "islands" in the river, poled the trees downstream with peaveys, making sure they didn't jam up and when they did, jumping aboard them and skillfully breaking the log jam apart. Logs were shipped around the country by rail and truck, and also overseas, becoming floors, furniture, masts for ships, telephone poles, toothpicks.

America used to be a land covered by old stand hardwoods, where vast forests stretched "from sea to shining sea" and trees and humans lived in balance. It was a land of plenty for everyone. We know this from history of the former native peoples, who numbered in the hundreds of thousands at one time, and from written accounts of the immigrant settlers of America. Trees were so plentiful that no one thought twice about coming to the end of this resource. Some forward thinking corporations began reforestation programs many decades ago, but mostly, trees were cut with no thought of tomorrow, all over the country.

One of the most important functions of trees is to hold the topsoil in place on the planet. Soil is a precious commodity, yet few people think twice about it. Bound together by a complex network of microbes, microscopic chains of nutrients, pulverized plant and insect remains, ashes from wild fires, rock powder, moss, lichen, it is sifted through, lived in, burrowed under, and rebuilt by the droppings of birds and small critters, worms and beetles. What a process! Trees and other plants anchor the soil, their leaves and branches providing mulch and cover for other species.

It takes at least one hundred years for one inch of topsoil to form, and only one second for roots to be ripped away. Unless covered, or replanted, the soil disperses; dig into it deeper with shovels or excavation equipment, and eons of planetary growth are gone with the wind. Government has always rewarded settlers, ranchers, farmers and industry for clearing the land. In the beginning, there were enough trees to go around. Not anymore. At this point, population growth has resulted in wood consumption that outstrips supply. This has dire consequences in terms of loss of habitat for trees and other existing species, as well as for humans.

Especially on the continents of Asia and Africa, and in rain forests all over the planet, trees are being impacted extensively by removal in vast swaths. Peoples' way of life is eliminated. Forests sustaining villages are gutted and the impoverished people—those who have not starved or died of disease—are relocated somewhere to shantytowns. Their food, medicine, shelter and income, linked inextricably to the trees, is gone. In most cases, forever. And eventually the entire ecosystem could be gone too.

If population expansion continues at the rate it is going, what will be the fate of the trees? Where will they live? And without trees, where will birds rest, nest and feed, where will pollinating insects and little critters burrow? From *Mother Earth News*, one of the only publications I subscribed to as a teen, comes a quote I memorized, by Eddie Albert: "The cycle is always the same: Man comes . . . the trees go . . . the topsoil goes . . . the desert comes. We are following that path."

In Colorado, I am talking with a land developer, who tells me his profession is purchasing small mountains around the country, for the express purpose of deconstructing them. He seems proud of the fact that every tree, mineral, boulder, and yard of soil is utilized—meaning sold off. There is no talk of a green belt, or reforestation. It seems that the elimination of habitat is not a problem. When I express concern over this, he emphasizes the benefit of a 20 unit low-income housing project, and short-term jobs in construction. Oh, and there will be a high dollar gated community and a golf course. Who benefits? If taking trees is done primarily for personal gain, my view is that it is unacceptable. Being the "owner" of the land doesn't seem to me to give a person the moral right to decimate it.

Yet, even the most conscientious of us does not entirely realize what we are doing with the land, and our daily use of tree products. Each of us comes from different backgrounds, yet some questions come up for everyone. Are paper bags from the supermarket better than bags recycled from plastic trash? How about coffee cups made from cardboard, phone books? Glossy publications on paper that will remain intact for decades in a landfill, are mailed by organizations claiming to be sensitive to the environment. And these are just the little things.

The truth is that we all overuse and abuse wood products on a daily basis. One thing I know is true for me: if I take personal responsibility for the role I play, if only a tiny part, I feel less powerless. There really is a lot I can do about righting imbalances, and the best way is right here in my own life.

Trees are life. It is a spiritual axiom that life is sacred, and to be valued. Once, we could live in balance with trees and all the other beings of the land. I think we have a spiritual responsibility to sustain all of life, not just the human part of it.

Written in 1624, John Donne's *Meditation XVI*, in *Devotions* resonates today:

> "No man is an island, entire of itself; every man is a piece of the continent, a part of the main. If a clod be washed away by the sea, Europe is the less, as well as if a promontory were, as well as if a manor of they friend's or of thine own were: Any man's death diminishes me, because I am involved in mankind: and therefore never send to know for whom the bell tolls; It tolls for thee."

HAVING A VOICE

Chapter Eight

HAVING A VOICE

 TREKKING IN THE mountains in Nepal, above Kathmandu on the way to Manaslu, something does not feel right. Then I notice that the hills are basically denuded. The last time I was here, birds sang, terraces gleamed in the morning and trees dripped with rain in the afternoon monsoons. Now, there is no song, because there are hardly any trees! I am crossing a landscape, changed.

Triggered by a late monsoon season, a gigantic mudslide, not more than two weeks ago, brought down the entire side of a hill. The over-forested land left no tree roots to hold the soil and rock in place. A terraced hill that once held trees collapsed upon an entire village, burying them in the middle of the night. Every living being in the village perished. I'm standing on what is now just a barren, flat, mud encrusted plain, scored by a slim trickle of water as the river carves a new path above ground. There is an eerie silence.

The next day, walking through heavily forested areas, I see trees being cut everywhere and transported out by yak. It is illegal to gather wood for resale without a permit. Yet, just like in America, it is not the individuals who account for most of the habitat destruction, it's big business: export. Very likely, this practice contributed to the mudslide that had dire consequences for the village of Macchu Kola.

There is a difference between cutting trees in a place like the mountains of Nepal out of necessity, and what is being done to trees elsewhere in the world to make room for urban development, especially when there are renewable sources of energy like sun and wind! Wood is still needed for survival, in the poverty stricken places on the planet. Villagers have no other source of heat in brutal winters, except ox dung, which only goes so far to warm a hearth and fuel the cook stove. The snow gets so high that long spruce poles with an identifying bunch of branch needles at the top, are planted next to a house in the countryside. This way, people are able to find their houses, coming back after being away in another village in a heavy blizzard. Living conditions are not easy, and they depend upon trees.

Our overpopulated world increasingly depends upon working together with greater awareness. However, nothing can be accomplished unless agendas are brought together through negotiation that benefits the many over the few. This principle of cooperation is perfectly illustrated by what happened in the village of Glen Haven, Colorado.

After several days of rain, a flood raised the stream into torrents. The soil, vulnerable due to the previous years' wildfires in 2012, did what any soil will do with no living roots to hold it back. It sloughed off, mixing into slurry, and poured downhill. Rampaging through homes, the flood uprooted vegetation, carrying boulders, vehicles, and everything in its path downriver in a torrent of churning, muddy water. Trees were tossed about and broken, and the little animals, birds, insects and plant life that used to live in them did not survive. It's a survival situation for the people too, and my mind is again on Nepal. But unlike that situation, there was warning, and the people were all evacuated. (No life was lost, they say—I guess by life, they are only thinking of humans.)

Soon, nature repairs itself. The trees that are left have become unbelievably healthy, two years later. Nutrients from the flood have replenished the soil. There is more room and light in which to spread and flourish, and new variety in the understory. The stream is cleaner than ever before in the aftermath of the flood. The water has purified the land. It reminds me that every disaster carries in it the seeds of regeneration.

Not only has most of the formerly flood-ravaged habitat rebounded, the road is repaired, the infrastructure restored, and the community is once again intact. No sooner has life settled down, when to my dismay, earth moving construction equipment is coming back into the area along the creek. My heart sinks, because construction disturbs habitat, tears up the ground, puts holes in the road, wreaks havoc with peace and quiet and creates chaos. The project concerns stream restoration, which is sorely needed in some other areas, but I think, not here. And my land access point is the one that makes the most sense for them to use because it will do the least damage to the overall habitat.

I'm worried, because humans have not done the best job thus far of protecting the environment or recognizing the importance of survival of species other than themselves. So I do what I usually do when I'm anxious. I seek out information. I talk with an optimistic, youthful administrative person, who says reassuringly, "All the agencies are going to work together to see that things that are damaged will be set to rights afterward." Not an encouraging statement. I wonder why this project is happening so late in the game.

Agendas are difficult to sort out because there are so many diverse factions and agencies involved. In addition to all the homeowners along the creek in question, there is a private not for profit environmental firm, a community resources council, and representatives from the town, the County, the State and the Fed. The project is extremely well thought out and the coalition has obviously put a lot of work into this. To their credit, they have followed due process to the letter. They are well intentioned, genuinely friendly and have bent over backwards to answer questions and arrange landowner meetings.

Their goals are: mitigate future erosion by placing boulders and net along embankments; prevent flood plain damage during spring run off; protect homeowners from damage in the event of another flood; restore native habitat; improve habitat for aquatic species of all types (fish, bugs, plants); add to the beauty of the area; and in general boost recovery so that the creek will heal itself.

My problem with the project is, simply, that nowhere in the prospectus is there any mention of trees, except for the idea of removing dead ones on landowner's property. Hundreds of trees have already been destroyed by the flood, and I am concerned that live trees that are seen as being in the way of the plan, will be disregarded. For example, a magnificent couple of old Firs were taken down in town on the county road (though not by this project.) They were removed because of being in the way of bulldozer access to the river during culvert replacement. No effort was made to move a few yards over, to save them.

This brings a memory of another place, another time, when a friend called me one evening, distraught. She returned from work to find that surveyors, hired by her neighbor, had chopped down the beautiful, mature, snow white birches along her property line, leaving high stumps bleeding sap in a long strip behind her house. It's not supposed to happen, but when it does, it is too late for the trees. So I worry that the trees left standing along the stream, may just be gone one day when I come home, if I grant access through my property.

My kinship with nature is sometimes stronger than my kinship with people who want to control nature. When there is another flood—which history shows there will be—no embankment solution will hold it back. Hoping to put my concerns to bed, I make a list of the good things that can come out of this project. I see that many of the coalition goals are the same as mine. When I meet with them, my voice on behalf of the trees will at least have been heard. Having a voice as a peaceful advocate for the trees is essential, if only in support of one's own health!

The fate of the trees depends upon many factors not under my control, and outside of my expertise. But there are many things each individual can do in the service of trees, and it is up to each of us to find our own comfort level with what this will be. In my view, some of the most difficult advocacy work involves finding collaborative solutions that give something to everyone, without destroying the habitat. Sometimes this takes years of negotiation on just one little item.

I think a lot about how to educate people who don't know that trees are living beings. I've concluded that it is a question of finding a way, through the obstacles, to bring in strategies that have widespread appeal. For example, everyone wants to live more healthfully, or so they say, and the health benefits of trees for humans cannot be refuted. Therefore, the fact that trees provide gigantic quantities of air filtration through the chlorophyll cycle might appeal, since there is evidence aplenty that the atmosphere of the planet is going to be irreparably damaged when the biomass drops below a certain point.

Consider how the air quality surrounding our planet would begin to change almost immediately by finding creative, affordable ways to make trees available to spaces that need them, especially in towns and cities. Perhaps this could be accomplished by exploiting what sells the image of trees; providing incentives for planting and propagation; getting civic and religious groups and local business involved in sponsorship; giving every single household around the world one free tree to plant and care for, and publicize it. These are a few things that could be done anywhere in the world to help trees have their voice.

Visiting Yellowstone Park, one of the Nation's first attempts to preserve nature from the predations of humans, I am happy to see the bison ranging there again. This iconic animal has been brought back from extinction in small herds; no matter that some of that motivation was economic—it's a start. Along with old stand trees, bison contain some of the spirit of the land, and of America. Emphasizing the benefits of reintroducing trees to our communities is just as crucial as reintroducing wildlife. The challenge for both is the same: how to do this effectively for the reintroduced species. Trees, as do wildlife, have distinct ecological niches within which they thrive—or they become invasive species.

But mostly, it's a question of how to engage the generations coming up, and this is best done with education, books, film, and true stories. When I moved to Maine, I bought a hundred mixed Evergreens as tiny twelve inch seedlings and saplings, and planted them, with help, in one backbreaking weekend. All summer I carried water down that hill and ninety trees made it. Today, a quarter century later, it's a veritable forest of gorgeous trees. And it was so much fun watching them grow up.

This story about the famous trade route, called the Silk Road from China to Europe, got my attention: Traders brought walnuts with them on the trip East. As they went, they dropped the nuts here and there. Years later, in their wake, hundreds of Walnut trees testify to the ease with which, given land that is undisturbed long enough for a seedling to sprout, a tree grows. Could it really be that easy?

Well, yes, it could. Little things make a difference. My mother reused and recycled everything. She refused to use paper towels and used the backs of bills for notepaper. My father, who made beautiful violins from curly Maple, loved the trees, because from the vibration of the beautiful wood, came music. Both of my parents valued books, and this showed me how to respect the paper itself, made from trees, where the words came alive. In other words, they taught me, by example, to honor the source.

Our children will inherit the Earth. With the raising of consciousness comes hope. Nobel prize winner, Wangari Maathai, was awarded a Peace Prize for her work helping women of Kenya plant and care for new trees, for which they received actual payment! It gave them not only jobs but introduced meaning to their lives by doing something to restore balance to nature. Reforestation cannot succeed without progressive, responsible social change. It's not just the fate of trees hanging in balance—it is the fate of humanity.

LEARNING

Chapter Nine

LEARNING

MY TEENAGE FRIEND and I are on a walk through the woods. He's a cool kid who just got a Bowie knife for his birthday, and he's trying it out on some trees. I'm alarmed, "Whoa, what are you doing with that?" He keeps right on, saying, "It won't hurt them." He is disbelieving when I tell him he is damaging the tree by cutting into its bark, so I give my 'trees are living beings' talk. Undeterred, his macho response is, "There are plenty more of them." I finally get it, he's showing off for me, and this is only bravado. He has since graduated from high school, a considerate and intelligent guy who does think of trees as alive.

This incident reminds me that despite having read Johnnie Appleseed as a child, I have done things that I am ashamed of concerning trees. I cut down a healthy young apple tree one summer day. My reason? This tree persistently attracted webworms, and I am afraid of them because when I was six, I was traumatized by the webworms in the Mulberry tree in our back yard, when a big glob of worms got into my hair and crawled on my face. It's still no excuse for cutting down a healthy tree.

Living for a quarter century in Holden Maine, surrounded by hundreds of acres of woods, I make little paths over the years. I congratulate myself that I use a handsaw, though I don't feel easy about cutting back saplings who struggle to grow in the thick, dark woods, reaching toward the sun wherever they can. I do it to make a path to accommodate me, the alien human in their community. Not something I am proud of, now. I guess I'm just human, like the rest of us.

Trees know if saws arrive in their midst. There is one Beech grove on the downhill slope in the thickest, darkest part of the woods that for years gives me goose bumps every time I pass it. Even the deer avoid walking through this place. The trees are gnarled and seem tainted. Most of the woodland Beech have blight, yet they grow to maturity relatively unaffected. However, The trees in this grove do not grow, they just barely hang on, their roots pushing above the ground in a thin tangle. I develop theory after theory concerning these problem trees. Soil pathology? A mineral vein running under in the dry streambed where they are located? Not enough water? An old graveyard with spirits in unrest?

Periodically, a forester goes down beyond the Beech line to thin the trees, mostly Evergreens, for firewood. The wood is stacked, cured for two years, and burned in the wood stove. Naturally, he uses a chainsaw. This is ostensibly for the health of the tree lot. It doesn't hurt, either, that it gives me a better view of the lake.

One day, I take a visiting friend who is a healer for a walk to the area in question, without telling her about the problem. As we come to the place, she says she senses something wrong, and surprises the living daylights out of me by turning to one of the trees, and asking, "What bothers you here?" And they tell her. Just like that!

She recounts what the one tree says, who speaks for them all. They seem to be a collective, they say, "We are afraid." They tell her that they witness their neighboring tree saplings being cut back every few years. Because they see me up the hill cutting branches off others of their kind with my handsaw, they identify me as the enemy. Every time I pass them they exude fear, and I feel it. They say they do not know me and think I am an intruder on the land. The solution, my friend says, is that the trees need reassurance from the "landowner" that they are safe. My friend says that the toxic biochemistry of their fear is killing them. Hard to believe? Here's what happened.

I decide to announce my presence to them by name as the caretaker of the land, and to reassure them that there will be no more cutting. Each time I go by, I address them, and each time the atmosphere lightens a little more. Sure enough, that summer they start to leaf out and eventually, they become healthier, though still blighted and stunted. Squirrels and birds re-inhabit them. When winter comes, deer move again among them.

And I feel better too. When I go by, I tell them my name and congratulate them on their improvement, and I put my hands on them and tell them I'm happy that we live in peace together on the land.

By making amends to trees that I hurt inadvertently, I can mitigate some of my mistakes. I now know that it is bad karma to cull healthy trees merely for one's own benefit. If it is truly for the health of the group, the greater good of the species, that's a different story. Yet, who gets to judge? It's sad how many of the things we humans think are necessary at the time, turn out not to be—such as creating a path through woods that were never meant to have one, or allaying a childhood fear.

Now I search my soul before I cut, and ask, "Is it necessary? And when I ask the trees directly, I always get an answer. From them, I learn discernment. Their message translates clearly into my awareness. The trees teach without words. Whether the answer comes from my higher self or from the trees themselves—probably both—it has proven to be a truer path than I could ever hope for from reliance upon emotion or ego, for a decision that means the difference between life and death of a living being.

BEING SEEN

Chapter Ten

BEING SEEN

IN NORTHEAST HARBOR, Maine, I am speaking with a bonsai Pine. The little tree bathes me in her serene wisdom as I sit by her side on a bench near a tiny, still pond. A barely discernable trickle of water finds its way down strategically placed rocks. The water is green, reflecting the willow tree draping itself gracefully overhead.

Everyone visits the Asticou Azalea Gardens from far and wide, and then has tea and scones with peach jam on the porch of the Inn looking out over one of the world's most famous anchorages. But few know of the secret other parts of the Garden hidden away nearby. While exploring ashore, I discover the other entrance quite by accident — though, of course, there are no accidents.

It is cool here in the midst of summer. Shadows sweep across quiet paths and rare, low-growing shade plants hide in corners. Light filters through the delicate burgundy boughs of a Japanese Maple. A sparrow picks through the groundcover.

I admire this little tree for a long time. Examining her careful beauty, entranced by the precision, yet ease, of her form, I wonder what it is that makes a person gravitate toward a particular tree. Is it the shape or location? The texture of the bark or color of the leaves? The presence or absence of flowers, berries or cones? The way that tree vibrates with one's own energy?

Lost in my thoughts, I hear a barely audible sound from the tree. She seems to be smiling at me, and I feel a glow around my heart. Her boughs dip softly and she says, hesitatingly, that she has "compassionate love" for those who sit nearby on the bench near the little pond. Then, a long silence. Most people can't endure even five seconds of silence without having to fill the space with speech. I value silence. It is so relaxing. Perhaps this is what draws me to her.

Not all trees evoke the same feeling. This little tree is full of love. She has a beautiful heart, vibrant, joyous. With this tree, I experience bonding. We sit in companionable silence for who knows how long. Then, coming to my senses, I feel that I have intruded. I turn to face her, apologize for not introducing myself, and ask her name. She tells me, "Noella." A lovely name.

Then, I ask her to tell more about compassion. She indicates that she feels compassion for those who pass by her without seeing her. She compares them with those who go immediately to her side. "Like me?" "Yes." I think, humans can learn from this tree about lovingly appreciating silence, feeling compassion for others who do not see. Such a gift I was given, to have found her. To then find a one-person bench just for me, by her side, hidden from view of the path and from passers by.

Usually, I embrace solitude. Today, I am lonely and long to share this beauty with another person who would understand who I am just by being. Yet, I have that experience more with trees than with humans. Perhaps it is because these finely tuned moments with trees require that I be alone to truly feel my own heartbeat. There is something about the energy exchange that happens only under these conditions.

When my ex-husband and I first met, one of the activities we shared is sailing. He kept a small sloop moored in Northeast Harbor, and we'd drive down from Bangor on Friday evening, car full of gear and a cooler, for an overnight weekend sail. Over the years, we often had a familiar discussion—with no real conclusion—about my desire to sail to some far away, new island, staying out as long as possible. His desire was to return early on Sunday afternoon to prepare for work the next day. Both of us worked full-time, but pragmatism took a back seat for me when it came to sailing. What is it they say: "Youth is wasted on the young?" In my case, it is, "Youth is wasted on trying to get my own way."

It is in an impatient frame of mind that I row ashore early Saturday morning in a huff, after another of these discussions, intending to drive up the road for a quick hike to clear my head. On a favorite trail in Acadia National Park, I pass through a grove of White Birch that grow near an underground stream. I have been here before, and have admired the trees' beauty. However, this time, a veritable wave of energy sweeps through the grove as I pass, yet there is no wind. The energy is buzzy and I feel lighter, happier.

On the way back along the waterfront, I stop in to see the little Japanese tree and we sit together in silent communion for a few minutes. When I row back to our boat, *Andiamo*, enlightened by the trees' healing energies, I am ready to compromise. My husband wants some time ashore, so we picnic on Schoodic Point that day instead of sailing. There is an inlet where wonderful rocks and all sorts of fascinating things appear in pools left by the outgoing tide. We have a different kind of talk—one in which we both feel acknowledged. We arrive home early enough for him to feel comfortable, and for me to enjoy a leisurely evening in the peace of my own garden.

The art of bonsai is an ancient Japanese meditation practice based upon aesthetic principles designed to evoke, and resonate with, feeling states. In bonsai, over many years, one learns patience, the principle that less can be more, and the value of letting things just be. One month, a snip here, another month, nothing, three months go by and a rock is moved into the habitat at the base. Sometimes an almost imperceptible change in the direction of a branch occurs over the space of a few years. I contemplate the parallel with human relationships that survive over long periods of time.

I ask a bonsai collector how he knows what to do, and he says, "The tree tells me." He says he receives clear, intuitive guidance from the tree about whether to do anything at all. Often, it is harder to do nothing, than to do something. Similarly, the caretaker at the Japanese Gardens, a slim young woman in a work study program in agriculture, says she listens to what the trees want her to do in terms of pruning. Yes, she has some knowledge of how to do things, but the main thing is to listen.

Concerning planting: a sapling often communicates to me, "put me here". Typically, I go ahead without further thought and put my spade to the ground right there. Rarely do I encounter obstacles. One time, I move a newly established sapling for my own aesthetic reasons. A few days later, I pass by and it insists, "Move me back." I do not see the problem until it tells me that it has too much sun in its new location. I put it back! Or, a tree that propagates by suckers, like an Aspen, might keep persistently growing over and over in the same inconvenient spot. Maybe it is a lesson for me in letting nature lead, so that I let my paltry little human plans follow their survival needs. Another lesson about human relationships.

The age of a tree gives it much time to understand about the human spirit. One day, I ask the bonsai Pine how long she has been here. I am shocked when she says, 75 years. She is a grandmother; I never knew mine. Maybe now I have met one. I return often over the years to visit, share silence and love, and I never mind driving the long way there.

PARALLEL LIVES

Chapter Eleven

PARALLEL LIVES

 PALM TREES ARE PERpendicular to the ground, as the tail of a hurricane sweeps across Abaco in the Bahamas. It's the day our movie company is shooting scenes on the beach, and we are on a schedule. Two days later, filming close ups at the only time the actors are available, the hurricane is past history and the palms are standing straight upright. Ordinarily, my job in script continuity would be to notice this kind of discrepancy, and the issue is that the long shots have to be combined with the close ups. We end up having to scrap a lot of the footage, and alter the script. The point that suddenly strikes me, reviewing the early footage that now cannot be used, is that nature is in charge of our movie.

There are remarkable parallels between humans and trees, both in terms of what both undergo in their lifespan, as well as behaviors in response to what nature throws their way. In the example of the Palm tree, there is the capacity to bend and in so doing, to withstand stress. Bend with the wind, or snap. Trees are beings adapted to their environment. They have the ability to flex when under pressure. Similarly, humans with this capacity, do well in life.

Exposed to harsh conditions, trees have the internal fortitude to protect themselves. They endure through great adversity. For example, in a severe ice storm, their entire body coated with a thick glistening casing of ice, yet they stand and deal with it. In the spring, they are almost always still alive. How is this possible in a winter storm that rages for a week, and takes out power for ten days! I think that trees go into some kind of stasis, or perhaps they pull back into their core. One could say that they minimize every non-essential expenditure of energy.

During times of adversity, it might seem that humans are more variable as a species than are trees. However, contemplating this, I realize that there are, again, parallels. Some handle stress with mental and emotional fortitude. For example, my cabin in Colorado is closely surrounded by mature, tall Pines and Firs. In a gale, the trees are subjected first to hail, then pelting rain. All night, the wind buffets, roars, lulls, roars again. Then, come morning, it is calm and sunny.

I go outside and see a mess that seems to have occurred down below near the stream. Several tall, spindly Spruce have toppled. Sometimes they just come unstuck from the ground when least expected. When they do, it can create a blow down, as one hits the other, like dominoes.

Laying on top of each other on the ground like pick up sticks, their shallow, round circles of roots are flipped onto their sides. I peer and poke around into the roots of the tree, hoping to find long hidden treasures embedded and now revealed. All I see is mud, clay, rocks, pebbles.

Looking underneath one of them after a hard blow that comes from different directions, it is a miracle that they grow so enormously at all, that's how shallow and relatively small their root structure is compared to their breadth and height. They are more vulnerable than Pines in the wind. Their shape is more symmetrical and therefore they present a more solid front against which wind exerts more force. With the Pines, the wind whistles through. I watch them in storms as they gracefully go to and fro, forward and back, over and over, with no apparent damage.

The human physique is like this. I whimsically imagine that tall, willowy pine-like people go with the flow; dense, stocky spruce-like people are firmer; palm-like people are flexible and spring back to center when put off balance. Those who adapt to their environments, survive. Some trees have such amazing survival abilities, especially in arid conditions, that they hang onto the bank of a river or stream with only a few roots sideways into the bank of a stream, twisted into shapes by the elements that make them take on a almost human form. There is one Cedar along Bear Creek in Gila that, to my eye, seems to be standing with her knee bent over one leg, like a Celtic dancer.

A tree's skin is like a human's. Infections or insects may get in through breakages or abrasions in skin or bark. Or, it may be too dry or scalded in the case of not enough rain, as human skin without enough moisture can become dehydrated and subject to burn. Blemishes and sores or cysts and moles may occur, or boluses. Some attachments are symbiotic and benefit each other. Even internally, the tree's circulatory system depends upon a free flow of sap, of phloem and xylem—the life blood of the trees. And humans? The veins and arteries are their transport system.

What about emotions? Trees can be stressed beyond their capacity just as can humans. Do they experience anxiety? I imagine their systems do. There is a psychophysiological theory in which a biological or genetic predisposition, in combination with continual stressors, eventually results in psychological imbalance. What if a tree is used to certain climates and conditions and, one year, it all changes. An uneven flow of energy occurs, when subjected to abuse or unusual weather or attack by insects. If trees are too crowded, disease is more likely as they are robbed of the nutrients, water and the very air that they breathe. Crowding affects humans adversely as well.

Do trees become depressed? Imagine how a tree's life force is intricately entwined with other non-human beings. Trees are used to being in a forest, woods or yard with others of their kind. Their roots touch—literally communicate—and their scents and pheromones mingle with all the critters, birds and insects that climb, perch and fly around, under and upon them. They depend upon one another, and all are in correspondence.

What happens to them when all of their kind are gone, and they stand alone in isolation? Wouldn't lack of connection with others of their species affect their health over time? Physiologically speaking, trees must have some awareness that neighboring beings, with whom they have been in close contact, are no longer nearby. My strong impression is that trees, like humans, are able to sense life present, so why not life passing. To say they grieve might be, for some, stretching a point. However, they surely do notice.

While walking in the woods with a friend, we go by an area that has been culled, the trees not yet skidded out of the forest. What is left of the grove looks healthy. Regardless of how well the remaining trees will do, now that there is not so much crowding, I cannot help but sense something about the spirit of the trees lying on the ground, dead or dying. We stop to pay attention to them, and while there, the inevitable question arises: When a tree dies, what happens to its spirit? Does the spirit pass immediately out of the body of the tree? With humans, it is said that the spirit stays close by the body, depending upon the circumstances of death, for some time.

Because of this question, I begin checking in on the energy states of trees that are newly felled. It appears that the spirit passes almost immediately from the tree. However, the body itself—the wood, and in the case of Evergreens, the needles—live on for quite awhile. And sometimes, depending on the species, regrowth occurs. Branches might bud out and eventually become new trunks. It takes a great amount of time, measured in our Earth years, for a tree to regrow. For some trees, as with humans, this is not possible.

Adversity, environmental conditions, crowding and over-population, loss of habitat and isolation, affect trees and humans alike. The characteristics of resilience and flexibility and adaptability are common to both. Maybe we are not so different.

LIVING TOGETHER

Chapter Twelve

LIVING TOGETHER

SITTING IN THE MAGIC circle of Junipers, near the stream under the Cottonwood with tea in the morning, I hear the wood rat sorting her treasures in a large disorganized wigwam of sticks built around one of the trunks. I imagine the snakes resting in the heat of the day in holes dug by gophers at the base. I see evidence of ground squirrels having gathered walnuts and sometimes hear their rustles. Birds come and go above. The lizards are the most fun to watch, as they dash in and out under leaves and brush, chase up and down branches, then rest motionlessly in what they think is camouflage, while they do pushups to cool down their bodies.

There are many old Cottonwoods along the Gila River. Once the water ran freely; now it is threatened by a dam and diversion initiative, along with the trees who depend upon the Gila. At one time, all animals went to the river to drink. Now they sneak into backyards, fenced off grazing lands, wherever there is water. It's in short supply down here in New Mexico. To have it at all, in the desert, is a gift. To lose it, a crime.

Those who come to live in Gila, are drawn by something inside of themselves that calls. Something off the beaten track. A little too hot and a little too remote for most people, I resonate with this land because of its resilience. Even though there is little rain most of the year, the vegetation adapts with a vigor that is astonishing. Plants who manage to get a foothold here, just keep on coming back no matter what.

To me, the Cottonwoods are the trees that epitomize the West. They live long and their thick branches spread out from a thick main trunk, like an Oak. Unlike hardwood, Cottonwood is light, much sought after by Hopi kachina carvers. But they become more easily water logged due to their habitat on the banks of rivers and lakes, and eventually rot at the base.

I knew an experienced, professional tree man who died taking down a Cottonwood in someone's back yard. Clipped on with his chainsaw, high up in the story, the branch gave way. His carabineer didn't release and he fell, with the limb, to the ground. I remember hearing him say, once, that he didn't like Cottonwoods because they rot inside and you don't know it.

Even knowing this about Cottonwoods, I still want to create a sitting area under a particularly gigantic one at the end of the property, bordering the confluence of the arroyo and the irrigation ditch. So, with a friend, I clear and clear one weekend. He saws and prunes. I pull and haul. The wildlife carry on their lives around me. I pull up Cochia and Mustard and Nettles by their roots, knowing they will be back in greater numbers next spring because I have distributed seeds into new crevices. Nature returns with a vengeance when and where it wants to.

For a while after that, one big old striped skunk persistently passes under my bedroom window every night for weeks, and sprays. I am sure he is getting back at me for disturbing his burrow. But then, it might have been the rains that came, washing him out. Happens every year. Then he finds a new burrow. I am sure that he is pleased with the big new pile of brush alongside his stream.

The old Cottonwood tree houses every kind of life imaginable. The fat branches hollow out easily and become home to those sheltering in, upon, under and around the vastness of this hundred year old being. I finally place two chairs in a clearing where a circle of stubby half buried Junipers are now liberated into sun. They love it. Their needles become a deeper green within days. I prune them carefully, with heavy gloves on, and they thank me for it.

Here, in the new clearing, I sit in contentment with a calm mind, entertained by a twig trying to get free of a jam-up in the flow of water in the ditch—what I euphemistically refer to as, the stream. Just as I glance away for one second, the twig is gone, and I have missed the big event. Or, I am practically hypnotized by a rock threatening to drop into the water from the gradually eroding bank. From my vantage point, I admire the ever-changing light on a slice of red and yellow mountain, across the fields where cattle graze. Sitting in the silence alive with sound, I hear the birds and insects talk, as I listen to the conversation of the water, wending its way inexorably toward the river. I am so grateful for this profoundly healing place.

Several weeks later, on my way out to my little clearing, something feels wrong. I don't see the chairs. I am momentarily disoriented. Then I see it: a three foot diameter branch has broken off and crashed down on top of both chairs, crushing them. The branch now lies across the stream, making a round slippery bridge. There was a high wind the night before. But still, I've been here long enough to never see a big part of that tree come down. Even the dog is stunned.

Does the tree not want me there? I did ask before moving in on her, if it was all right. Prior to clearing the little sitting area, she seemed friendly; now she is kind of standoffish. Maybe I didn't inquire carefully enough and just went ahead and did what I wanted to do there, under her gaze. My presence did scare off a black hawk who used an abandoned nest in the highest and most concealed V as a perch. (The hawk merely relocated to the next Cottonwood down the way). Perhaps the Cottonwood is afraid of being felled. Because, one by one, they are being taken down. Does my Cottonwood know? She is within line of sight of cleared land that once was home to a proud row of her kind. She must have felt the vibration of her companions falling not an eighth of a mile from her.

Cutting away the chairs from under the crashed branches, I find a small metal sign on the main trunk that I had not seen, covered up as it was by smaller branches. It says, " NEIN". I am puzzled because no former owners were German. Is it a warning to not cut this tree? Or does it refer to tree number nine—there are at least that many

Living Together

old ones along this arroyo— and is simply misspelled? I ask around town, and no one has any ideas. It's a mystery.

So, instead of sitting near the water, I retreat back to sitting under the portico of my little adobe house, where I can still see the Black Angus graze. It's spring in New Mexico and the cows are calving. There are lots of little babies out there cavorting and lots of mom's bawling for them when they stray. Just like humans. The family dynamics right there for everyone to see.

The portico is hung with the bones and antlers of critters found by my ex-partner cowhand. He has an uncanny ability to find things that I pass right by. One, a five point Elk skull and antlers, he found more than a mile from my cabin in Colorado, and dragged back down a mountain in the middle of winter. Many are hung on the portico posts. It's funny how many people immediately bond with me, when they see that, assuming I am a hunter. I hate to disappoint, but I'm no hunter. Red the Wonder Dog's special ability is finding rabbits, but he's too slow now to catch anything. Everyone has a special intuitive instinct for finding something in nature. I find plants.

It's time for the irrigation ditches to be cleaned out. Carl does this for the whole area, it's one of the coveted few jobs that actually pays anything around here. His old farm machines are in perfect condition. In these parts, irrigation is essential, for this is an agricultural community. The first year I lived here, he bulldozed over a Willow tree along my stretch of the ditch. I was upset, and blurted out, "It's so hard for them to grow here." He said, with a straight face, "Their roots are in the way." I can see where it is annoying to the local inhabitants, when someone "from away" moves into town and thinks she knows something. People are too polite to tell me that things have always been done this way for a reason. It's not so much resistance to change—it just might be true that things work better the old-school way.

In another place, another time, when I first moved to the woods, the locals laughed at me for spending hours removing dead wood from the woods, piling it up at the edge. "There'll just be more of it later", my neighbor said, scratching his head, probably thinking, "These city folk don't know nothin'." I think that I am doing something useful, taking care of the trees, by tidying them up, and because the branches rub onto each other in the wind. Later, I find out that trees actually communicate with each other this way, and that it is I who did not understand.

DARK FOREST

Chapter Thirteen

DARK FOREST

STANDING VERY STILL on top, seeing for miles, nothing in sight but sky, and trees. My heart rate slows from the climb up Cathedral Trail to the summit of Maine's famous Mt. Katahdin, northern end of the Appalachian Trail. When the scudding clouds part, and it is light enough through mist to look down into the valley, all the trees that claimed my attention individually on the way up, now seem to be an undifferentiated ocean of green.

They are mostly Evergreens, and they are moving. I realize how they adapt to the rhythm of the wind, the bird who lands, the squirrel who runs along a branch. They are not stationary, they bend and sway in response to other living things, as if none are separate. It is all one moving, interrelated pulse of life. I think this is what is meant by, "We are all one."

It's such a long climb in one day—12 hours—that I give myself only a half hour on top, so I can get down before dark. I don't want to try Knife Edge in this weather. Truthfully, I have never tried it, no matter what the weather. It is really true that in some places there is no more than a foot and a half with a sheer drop on either side. My climbing does not include much real climbing, it's more like scrambling endlessly. Being five foot two does not help. One time I was stuck spread-eagled on a face, climbing up to The Owl, and it took everything I had to hang there until someone came along and boosted me. A rock that I planned to step down on decided to drop off when my foot touched it. I'm not really a rock climber either . . .

Reluctantly, I start the long way down, on Saddle Trail. It thunders, in distant growls, despite a clear weather report. I am encouraged that, below the slide, I can see the crooked scrub growth called krumholtz. Great word. I have reached trees, that's something. It has gotten suddenly cold, and the storm is coming on fast. I have never once been here when it has not done something like this, no matter what time of year, or forecast. Here comes the lightening.

I can never remember the correct protocol for not getting struck by lightning in the wilderness. Is it, "never stay out in the open," or "get down under the tree line", or "make sure your body is always lower than the highest tree?" I suspect that the fact that I cannot form an opinion means that I am getting hypothermic, but I don't know what to do about it, which only confirms my theory. So, I do what not to do in a lightning storm. I sit on the ground, take off my pack, and burrow close to the trunk of a tree, under its boughs, into the needles at its base.

It is July, and starting to rain. I have put on everything I have in my pack, but am still cold. I go out of body to pass the time. Trees are so friendly. I feel protected by the pulse of this big being—lulled into complacency by the regular drip of the rain from the branches of the tree. It's like a metronome set on slow. The light is fading to gray. Some part of my brain is functioning, though, and I know that I can't stay here long. I need to get moving. Now.

Back on the trail, I go for about a mile, though it seems longer. It doesn't look familiar. This is my fourth time on the mountain and I'm pretty sure I know what has happened. I think that I have gone off to the West along a ridge that leads to another peak. Something about blueberries there sticks in my mind, from having seen smears of blue on the ground left by bears, another time near the descent from Chimney Pond. I have to admit I am lost. Wishing that I had not decided to hike alone, I console myself with some trail mix. One of the big disadvantages to hiking alone, is that there is no one with whom to discuss things that go wrong. Rain, no sun, late in the day, I have lost time on this mistake. That isn't good.

I've never been good on directions, and though I do have a topo map, my compass is malfunctioning. Something magnetic must be interfering. I look all over in case there is a meteor around somewhere, an idea that makes me laugh out loud. It's nice to hear my voice. I look for the Big Dipper so I can line up with the North Star, but it's still too early. Then I decide to try to climb a tree to get my bearings. That tree is so slippery and the branches so far apart that I can't get more than ten feet off the ground before I slip off. This seems to knock some sense into me, and I realize that I have not once thought about engaging my intuition. Just realizing this brings in the idea that I must have missed a trail marker. Backtracking methodically, I find it. The storm is rolling away, rumbling as it goes, and now it is raining hard. But at least I know where I am.

It is dusk, not my favorite time to be hiking alone, and I still have some ground to cover. I turned off my feelings a few hours ago, so I'm not feeling much except the instinct to go fast and not stop. I talk to myself, sing, and make some noise. The soggy ground swallows me up time and time again as I trip on roots and skid off boulders. My boots are made for this kind of thing, but it's at the point where it doesn't matter. Sometimes I recognize a tree. Finally I get to the easy part, only a couple of miles to go. I'm guided to my truck by the unerring instinct of a homing pigeon. lucky to not have twisted an ankle or something worse.

Eventually, back around 8 at night just before dark, on the trail since 6 that morning. Feeling like a poster child for what not to do when hiking, I sign out sheepishly. The ranger says that she was just about to go out looking for me. She asks whether I have passed a family with two kids, on my way down. They set off late in the day, planning to camp. I say I haven't seen them. (The rangers can warn hikers but they can't enforce anything if the hiker is not breaking the law.) She tells me that she is going to have to go out and find them, eyeing me while commenting that, "The forest is dark at night." I nod in agreement, while seriously contemplating this statement.

Rescue personnel endanger their lives for people who make foolish decisions. Like me, hiking without a partner! When I am in the Italian Alps one year on a road trip, I talk with a ranger who has just returned from a rescue mission. He sounds bitter, saying, "these people expect us to save them when they do things they are not aren't supposed to do." In this case, it is a couple who wander off into an inviting looking forest and end up on a glacier. One of them falls and is badly injured. They were lucky to have a cell phone. The rescue costs the Regional Mountain Service the equivalent of $10,000.

One of the least visible rescue jobs, and one I greatly admire, is dealing with the wildfires that rage year after year through the forests. Agencies of all sorts coordinate, plan, fight, clean up, and monitor fires. At one time, fires were part of the natural balance of nature, and the land could absorb the losses, and benefit. There was so much land, so many trees, relative to people. Overpopulation has changed all that, now, at great cost to trees.

I live in a canyon, at 7500 feet of elevation, protected by trees on all sides. On one side is a wilderness area with nothing between me and Wyoming to the north, and on the other is National Forest. It is a very dry, thickly forested area, with deep, friable duff and evergreen needles everywhere. We're in a drought. One late summer day, someone didn't extinguish a campfire properly. I notice haze and smell smoke, and it stays like that for weeks, due to a wildfire burning in Rocky Mountain National Park, ten miles away. Planes drone overhead and black helicopters patrol.

One day, hiking, I run into some guys who look like firefighters, and they tell me there are new conditions. "The fire jumped a ridge in high winds during the night and is coming down the mountain, this way." I say, "How fast?" They aren't worried. So, that evening, I go back out and watch as the flames turn to smoke when the planes dump water, then spring back up. If it were not so horrifying, it would be beautiful, the sky lit up with orange.

I try not to think about the trees bursting into flame, and the critters running panicky to try to escape. Most of the little ones, who cannot burrow deep enough, don't get out. What of the amphibians and fish? The birds? People say the deer, elk, mountain lions and bears always get out, but that's not what I hear, because, as I learn later, wildfires can suddenly cut off escape routes by veering in unanticipated directions. A dull ache starts up in my solar plexus and won't go away.

The next morning, the firefighters are going door to door telling us to get ready to evacuate. We are told we have 24 hours, but are advised to leave immediately. I go through the interesting process of deciding what to pack into my car. My dog, of course. My away kit, always ready. My father's violins and one possibly valuable painting which, with my luck, is more likely a forgery, or it would have been sold off by my family long ago. My sleeping bag. Boots. Fleece. My computer. Some cans of my favorite imported tuna. Jewelry. Mr. Rabbit. A few books, but, which ones? Hours go by while I pass the time reading some old sci-fi novellas, and looking at hundreds of photographs. Finally, I am ready. I get into my sweats and sit in my car.

That night, the evacuation is called off. The fire has been 80% contained about a quarter mile from my cabin. The personnel work for months more, because the containment comes and goes. The following year the fire, smoldering in two feet of duff, breaks through again. By then, though, they are ready for it.

From this and other examples, my eyes are opened concerning what it is that government agencies do for the public. The Forest Service office in Walden, Colorado is a firefighter marshaling station for the Medicine Bow-Routt National Forest. As an employee for a half year, I am required to watch a terrifying documentary about the 2013 wildfire in Arizona that claimed the lives of nineteen men and women from the Granite Mountain Hotshot Unit. I talk with someone involved in the mobilization of the rescue effort. Though the deaths of the people are unbearable enough, I ask him about the wildlife. He averts his eyes and shakes his head.

According to the U.S. Dept. of the Interior, ninety percent of wildfires are caused by humans, not by lightening. Trails are closed sometimes for years because of the danger of snags falling, and it takes decades for trees to grow back. After a fire, the forest is dark—blackened, lifeless. Mountainsides and meadows stand in misery. Then, the understory rebounds, miraculously. The soil is strengthened and nourished by the organic material from the burning. Baby seedlings are fertilized by the dead trees, merely two years later. New life.

I don't think people are really aware of the job emergency teams do to rescue people, and what rangers and foresters, biologists and recreation personnel do for trees. True, the bureaucracy is unbelievable to work with. Everyone has to cut through masses of red tape and legalese in order to get anything done. Just keeping people from illegally cutting trees in protected forests could be a full time job. Lives are saved in ways that are not generally known.

Danger is inherent in wildness. Nature will do what it does, with or without us. It would be wise to respect it, rather than to try to tame it. We like to think that we are in control of nature, that we can discern what is best for the planet, but the dark forest will relentlessly continue on, with or without us. It has lessons to impart concerning survival—if we listen.

MUSIC OF MIGRATION

Chapter Fourteen

MUSIC OF MIGRATION

A SPOT OF RED FLIES across the field into a tree, then ten, then staggered battalions of hundreds more. It is a late fall November morning, ground grasses still standing stiff with frost. The birds are on the move. They're right on schedule. Migration spells the end of fall and the onset of winter where I live. Flying in straight lines close to the ground, they head for the trees.

Trees provide protection for many, but never in such a spectacular way as for the birds. As I reach for the binoculars hanging next to the door, I speculate about who this mob is. I'm not a pro, so it takes me awhile to even find them through the branches in the binocs, glasses scrunched against my eyes while fighting for focus. Finally I see one clearly, just the head, in color, and it's not one I know. Too big for pine siskins, too small for robins. And those aren't migrating now. Not likely to be a mob of woodpeckers, are they? Do they migrate? I'm all over the map. Towhees, that's it! In the fifteen seconds it takes me to sort through this diagnostic mess, they have moved on.

I was alerted to the relationship of trees to birds early in my life, by my grandfather who was what is now called, a birder. I have his folder of original Audubon prints to this day. What he did that was unusual, was to point out the trees that certain birds liked, and he would speculate why that might be so. And could he ever whistle those bird songs!

I became more interested in birds when I began to see them flying over my rental cabin in Middle Island, New York. I turned to watching them for respite from studying and working three jobs at one time, while in graduate school at Stony Brook. My lifelong trend of living in the woods, in cabins, began here. Noteworthy for housing the World's Fair Scandinavian exhibit in 1939, the cabin was purchased by the landlord's father for his bride, and transported by a team of oxen into what was then, wilderness. The cabin was made of cedar, which didn't stop it from being eaten by carpenter ants; I could hear them chewing near my head in the bedroom wall. There, I escaped being crushed to death by a large Maple who came down during a storm along that same wall, one night. I felt a great shudder of the cabin that briefly woke me. When I went out in the morning, the trunk of an enormous tree was laying along that wall not more than a foot from it.

This cabin is perfect for migrating birds: large lake nearby, cemetery and golf course across the road. It is

Music of Migration

positioned exactly under the flight plan for hundreds of migrating birds, along a major East Coast corridor. Here, they can take a breather on the first leg of their long voyage south. I hear them coming from miles away. They form a thick, dark swath overhead, obscuring the sky, covering the sun. Day becomes night. Migrating boat tailed grackles deafen with their cawing. When they fly at night, waking me, I run outside and feel, not see, them passing overhead. Sometimes they are so thickly packed up there that their wings create their own atmospheric breeze, like a gentle wind, that goes with them as they fly into the distance. Sometimes thousands at a time will take an hour to pass.

The seemingly impenetrable mass of sound is so distinctive that I can still summon it up now — it's wild! The sounds of the geese are spectacular. This is the true meaning of the phrase, cacophony of sound. Sometimes I can pick out individual calls, depending on the species migrating. I wonder what they are saying. Are they joyously speaking about the freedom of flight? Calling out to gather up every one of their species on the way? My theory is that they are sounding warnings, like a car honking its horn to prevent its being run into, letting all other life in the sky know that they are roaring through. Watch out! Maybe they are giving directions, screeched at top volume: "See down there, a grove of strong trees, no wires in the way, a pond, a field with grain seeds, reeds, grass, good cover." I can just hear them talking about it.

Sometimes they decide to land smack dab in my yard, and in that case, I don't dare be in the middle of that organized chaos. They are everywhere, hopping around, decimating the remains of my garden, on the roof, on an overhead electric wire. What did they do before electricity?

Doves especially seem to position themselves equidistantly up there. Ospreys like to build nests on the tops of those poles. They must like getting a buzz. But mostly, they are in the trees.

Every branch is covered, sagging, dark with birds. They come in relays and suddenly, for no discernable reason, they whoosh away, wings beating a noisy return to the sky. In their stead, immediately come another several hundred of them. The big ones break branches. Sometimes there are smaller birds, like finches, or grosbeaks, who are pretty heavy on the trees too. The really little guys, the sparrows, stay mainly the ground or flutter up and down looking for food. The soil benefits from all those droppings!

Seems as though every place I live is on a migration path of some kind. Maine, Colorado, S.W. New Mexico—each place brings an entirely different set of birds. Recently, I had the great good fortune to live on a migration path, near a bird sanctuary. Now mostly working from home, it is easy to become involved in the daily rhythm of the birds' lives and their relationships to trees. I even purchase a new pair of binoculars to replace the ones destroyed in protest, by Princess Blueberry, the new puppy. I think she was trying to tell me she wanted to go out.

With increased opportunity to observe the daily lives of birds in trees, and their energetic interface more closely, I see that there is some kind of higher-order relationship between trees and birds. It makes me wonder if they might not need each other for a purpose more elevated than a mere perch for singing. Of course, I know that the uses of trees for birds are myriad: mating and migrating perches, nesting and feeding stations. It's clear how birds are helped by trees. But I cannot come up with much on how trees are helped by birds. Do trees welcome birds? So I decide to ask them. And I get the usual diverse set of responses.

The Pines seem a bit annoyed, which surprises me. Though, in general, they tend to support fewer birds at one time, usually a lone crow or warbler on the very top, calling out from the tallest perch. They like white breasted nuthatches, who beep as they hop, upside down, along the trunks. The Spruce, Cedar and Juniper indicate that they like having little birds snuggle into their narrow spaces between prickly branches, huddle there, build nests, sing. Chickadees, sparrows, wrens, orioles. The trees express concern about the nests being destroyed by marauding blue jays and their budding pinecones being gnawed by squirrels. In fact, most trees do not seem to like squirrels, who act as if they are entitled to being anywhere they want, without regard for anyone else.

Smaller fruit trees and ornamentals enjoy birds in a playful way. They see themselves as beautiful, so the birds' exotic beauty mirrors their image of themselves. They enjoy the show. However, the big fruit and nut trees, like Apple and Chestnut, are not that thrilled with birds. They are upset by seeing their fruit damaged by certain birds, though most leave the fruit alone. They shelter robins, harbingers of spring, and cute little tufted titmice.

Tall bushes welcome nesting birds. They love sheltering a flash of blue of a rare warbler or bluebird, the yellow of a goldfinch, orange of a tanager passing through. And they like having their clever, basket nests hung high when they leave. The songs of quail, marshaling hoards of babies following their bobbing scrolled heads under

Spirit of Trees

bushes, are wonderful. Bushes have big issues to worry about, like being trimmed all the time, or rampaged through by a small herd of peccaries. One group is indifferent, those with thorns.

Hardwoods, like Oak and Maple, are more accepting, which is to be expected. Their big spreading roundish, mushroom-like shapes support many migrating birds. They have a more expansive view and lofty things to think about, so they don't mind birds coming and going all the time in their branches. Especially along rivers like the Gila in New Mexico—one of the only rivers left around that is still untouched by dams— the Cottonwoods look like they are going to break, they are sometimes so heavy with birds. Their branches, touching, leafing out, provide a canopy for migrating birds. Listening to the complicated and beautiful music of the warblers and finches who land there in the spring, is thrilling.

The big trees are home to the big birds. Hawks do touch-and-go landings, and search for prey from the strangely shaped branches of Cottonwoods. Trees that support eagles are proud of it. Seems to be a spiritual relationship. I have the impression that big birds are necessary for them, though I couldn't say exactly why. It might be stimulating for them, kinesthetically, to have birds bouncing on them. Magnificent are the Sandhill Cranes. They don't stay long, but while they are here, it is one of the highlights.

Woodpeckers get a varied reception from trees. Some trees are happy to be pecked into, much like a water buffalo is happy to have egrets sitting on his back, removing the pesky insects. Some are too weak and therefore get a bit wounded by pecking. Some feel good to have woodpeckers and owls sitting in their cavities, making a home.

Trees have a wary relationship with crows and their trickster ways: clever and watchful, and intelligent! Highly social, at times too much so, they seem to have a complex family life in not one but several trees at once. The Evergreens support them well. Ravens are my favorites, with their complex guttural sounds of clicking and gronking. The vultures, revered in many cultures, fill an important role in cleaning up the environment. It's a heavy tree or snag that supports them, that's for sure.

Birdfeeders, while not exactly a tree, somewhat mimic the real thing, and provide dinner too. The birds who frequent the feeders are another story all together. It's a complicated dance, hoards of migrating birds swooping onto feeders and decimating the contents, spilling some onto the ground for juncos and ground feeders to have their fill. At the feeders, all talking at once, they sound like an orchestra tuning up before the concert.

All trees tell me they like the little hummingbirds very much, and their delicate little baskets hanging off a branch. These amazing birds migrate several thousand miles each year, over entire oceans. Many have become dependent upon feeders. Like migrating ducks and geese, they have specific stopping places as they travel, or they drop from fatigue. How will they fare if a forest they counted on last year for their rest stop is simply not there anymore? They need trees for their survival.

The birds come and go, yet the music remains. From a family of musicians, I had music in my head from the moment I am conceived, and before that! I can usually remember a musical phrase or entire song if I hear it only once. I run for the bird books and look for bird songs, when I hear a bird song I don't know. Oh, the music! I understand. This is how birds benefit trees! Music is sound, sound is life, vibration, energy. Birds make music for themselves, yes, but also for the trees, who are stimulated by the vibrations. On a spiritual level it rings true.

CONCRETE PARK

Chapter Fifteen

CONCRETE PARK

IN NEW YORK CITY, Washington Square Park is home to concrete chess tables standing beneath the shade of trees. All sorts of strange bedfellows play chess, from amateur to expert, and there's always a crowd looking on. The trees seem to watch too, giving the game a feeling of solemnity and dignity, while dogs and students move about, play frisbee, talk, read, and lie around on blankets spread on the almost grassless ground. People play with the babies and try to keep a rein on the kids, and old people sit, visit, doze. Business people pass through carrying briefcases on their way to Fifth Avenue. Homeless people love this park. It has a sense of community.

However, Central Park is what everyone thinks of when trees are mentioned, and indeed, it is an old and beautiful park, especially in autumn. Magnificent because of its antiquity, it even has a lake with overhanging Willows. And because of trees, there are birds and all sorts of critters there. Unfortunately, it is not the safest to walk there alone in daylight, much less at night. Yet, I did that almost every day. I guess I was lucky—I never got mugged in New York—only in other cities, though I had more close calls than I want to remember.

Most people walk or bicycle, without money for cab or car, to school and to work, and stay pretty much in their own neighborhoods when they get home. Mine was the upper West Side. There, I went to High School at Professional Children's School, and received my Undergraduate degree at Columbia University. My first apartment was in Greenwich Village near Washington Square, and then on West End Avenue near Riverside Park.

The trees in New York City instill in me a feeling of security, a built-in response to having a living being nearby who is not part of the onslaught of rushing humans one constantly encounters. Not part of the potential danger of humans, trees are safe and definitely more approachable. Even though the dirt under each tree is usually flattened into hard pan and littered with cigarette butts and food containers, just seeing and feeling trees in the midst of any city, makes me slow my pace. I can look up, take a deep breath, and feel myself relax. Each tree is important in a city of millions of people, surrounded by concrete, metal, glass.

Sometimes I see trees growing out of the tops of apartment buildings. Actually, those are penthouse gardens, completely out of reach for any but the rich folks. The regular folks have to be content with the few trees they can find on the streets. One of the trees seen everywhere is what we, on the block, call Gingkos, known for their ability to survive pollution and general abuse. They have an unpleasant odor when stepped on, and they just keep coming back.

Years later, I find out that many of them are not Gingko at all, but a tree I am familiar with from the Southwest United States, euphemistically called the Tree of Heaven, Elianthus. It can be a veritable plague, crowding out other saplings, spreading through an underground lateral root system, relentlessly drinking water and storing it in a large bolus that feeds it during times of drought. However, birds like them, and their leaves and racemes are lovely.

They have taken over a mostly cement park downtown on Houston Street, in Little Italy near where I lived before moving uptown. There's a basketball court that doubles for tennis and handball, sturdily surrounded by tall wire fencing. Not exactly pretty, except that around it exist several of these indestructible Elianthus trees. It is the tree made famous in the story, A Tree Grows in Brooklyn—just the thing for a concrete park. Trees in multi-use parks have to work to get a foothold and to stay alive, because they are subjected to abuse. People carve initials in their bark, break off branches, and the dogs sure do a number on them. One has to appreciate their stoicism and their adaptive abilities.

In order to get to my favorite park of all, I take the bus uptown on Sunday morning, first stopping at Barney The Sturgeon King, for a bagel and lox and a coffee. It's a long way up to The Cloisters, and it feels like I am going on vacation. Located above Columbia Presbyterian Hospital, where I was born, near the Washington Bridge, is a belt of green, and the Medieval branch of the Metropolitan Museum of Art. With the weekend edition of the New York

Times, I sit on the grass outside this ancient reconstructed cloister, amidst the oak trees. Chants are piped into the garden area, bringing beauty and calm. The stones echo, and the spirits of the trees surrounding it are strong.

There are other parks, more beautiful, in other cities where I have lived. In Paris, right outside the apartment loaned to me by a friend, is the Jardin du Luxumbourg. I could never afford it otherwise. It's something out of a painting—the French sure know how to do a park! Wide tree lined paths, architectural gardens, overhanging Willows. Nannies pushing strollers, just like they did a hundred years ago. Yet, just like in New York, people sit on benches in all kinds of weather, with coffee and baguettes, feeding the pigeons.

There's nothing like a big city to make a person appreciate trees! Being in the aura of trees is why people living in cities go to parks. They may not realize it, but they crave the energy of this living being who, slower paced and patiently enduring the cycles of the seasons, helps them to slow down too. They often sit with their backs against the trunk of an old tree. It's a secure feeling in an insecure world.

SAMSARA

Chapter Sixteen

SAMSARA

My town is out of the way, by most peoples' standards, yet the drive home is worth it. Thirty five miles from the nearest place to buy groceries, through wide open rangeland, there is often not one vehicle in sight. I pass farms and small ranches with horses, and cattle dotting the fields, green with alfalfa, And wide yellow flats of yucca below multicolored hills rearing up in layers. Nearing town, past the transfer station, across the wash barely running with a trickle of mud. Past dusty front yards of Cholla and Prickly Pear Cacti, broken down vehicles, parts of farm equipment, discarded sofas and kid's toys. Past the 1970's trailers and the modulars, neatly stuccoed to look like adobes with neat turquoise trim.

Hey, there is some activity in the center of town—a few cars are in front of the post office and the senior center—must be noon. Two weeks of being away from here, I am full of joy to see the sun on the hill shining gold, like Coronado's fabled cities, at the end of my road. I take a deep, clean, satisfying breath. Home. I stop in for mail and then at the library housed in a trailer with its amazing tile mural portraying a rearing horse of beautiful colors, under the little covered porch. Across the street is a closed down village store, and a purple adobe building adorned with fanciful sculptures and of snakes and lizards. Passing the community clinic, a forgettable small white building, I see something green, and screech to a halt in the parking lot.

Trees! I see trees, where there was formerly only a parking lot filled with sand, broken rock and the usual variety of unidentified sticker plants. A sign says that this is the Gila Valley Community Forest, a collaborative effort of the Gila Valley Library, Aldo Leopold Charter School, Amma Center of New Mexico, and Hidalgo Medical Services. Filling an area no bigger than a small backyard, this tiny forlorn space is now transformed into living beauty. The forest, actually a garden with trees, is funded by a demonstration grant from the New Mexico Energy, Mineral and Natural Resources Department, and the U.S. Department of Agriculture Forest Service.

There were three such grants offered to communities in New Mexico, and the only one that materialized was here in Gila. One was given back to the State because it didn't have anyone to administer it on site, and another was declined due to lack of interest! Who would decline such a gift, for such a cause? Anyway, there are two thousand dollars with which to buy everything needed to establish a forest. This sounds like a joke, doesn't it? The money is for seedlings, trees, irrigation equipment and materials, cement, tools, signage and whatever else goes into making a shoestring project, matching grant, happen.

This is no ordinary gardening project. But then, Gila is no ordinary place. Eric Leahy, a professional landscaper, and all around plant person, volunteers to spearhead the effort. When he is not ordering trees and plants from anywhere he can get them, he and the few other adults who volunteer, haul local stones and boulders, transport containers of trees and plants from Silver City, pour concrete, build terracing, and dig holes for trees and trenches for irrigation pipe. Eric says his main inspiration comes from time over the years spent at an ashram in India, working with the land, giving time with no expectation of return. "Trees want to be planted," he says with a happy smile, looking around.

It could not have happened without the volunteer kids, especially the Aldo Leopold High School, and the Montessori School in Silver City. I ask Eric if he has a plan or blueprint that the volunteers follow. He shrugs noncommittally, saying that the project unfolds as an organic process in which availability of help determines the outcome of where things are planted, not a landscape architectural plan. He works alone a lot on the project, but all of a sudden there's an influx of 20 kids, and things that happen to be there, get planted. It looks like it is orchestrated, and the effect is electrifying.

Bordered by a stone wall, a winding cement path, and eighty newly planted trees, in just three months a wasteland has been transformed into a young forest, with an understory consisting not of the usual boring bushes commonly seen in mall parking lots, but unusual flowering perennial plants, herbs and bushes. Some of them are already spreading and reseeding. The seeds will be saved and made available to the Gila Valley community for planting in their own spaces too. Low lying Thyme spills over the wall and sturdy Echinacea and furry little Lambs Ears thrive under small trees. Interspersed are flowering bushes of Coryoptera and Plum, their roots intermingling to hold moisture and share nutrients. They literally commune with one another.

There are Redbuds and Golden Rain trees, Pecan and Fig and Persimmon, Locusts and Sycamore, and all sorts of Evergreens including an exotic Japanese Spruce. A suggestion from the power company to remove an elegant Pine, who has already been moved once because of being erroneously planted on top of a leach field, will be taken care of instead by gently bending it to the side over time, so that it will completely miss the overhead line if it gets to growing in that direction. There is always another way.

The plants around the health clinic will help clients to heal more quickly. Research shows that when people brush up plants, essential oils, pheromones and the healing qualities of specific plants are communicated. And they are psychologically and emotionally healing as well. Along the foundation of the stark white undecorated building of the clinic, there are fragrant, healing herbs of Rosemary and Sage. Breathing in produces a deep relaxation response, softening the tensions in the entire body. All the senses take in the beauty.

Butterflies, hummingbirds and bees pollinate the community. Birds and other little creatures—including the much maligned gopher—are already in residence. Next summer the small fruit trees will bear flowers to feast eyes upon and yield fruit for patients to pick. There is a place to slowly stroll and sit and just be. Stress dissipates, as I walk in the very young and already bountiful places created outside the clinic walls.

What is striking about the new plantings is their vibrant health. No commercial chemical or even organic fertilizer is used here. One scientific reason is that the trees, especially, must put down their roots in this habitat, unaided. This is a harsh climate, with temperature extremes typically swinging fifty degrees in the space of one day. If the trees are jump started as youngsters with fertilizer, an artificial growth spurt is created, that prevents their roots from being tough enough to integrate with base soil. Trees do best if put in the ground and allowed to settle naturally into the rhythms surrounding their living space. Provided with the most basic elements that nurture them—earth, air, water and metal—and combined with the chemistry of their neighbors, they will put down their roots firmly, and flourish.

However, there is something in addition to biology going on here with this project. It is the energy of the individuals creating this space that fosters the health of the trees and plants. I especially like the fact that someone had the grand vision of its being called a forest. In some circles, this is called "manifesting" with intent, or creation of form through the action of harmonious vibration. By meditating in the presence of the trees and plants—sending love, beaming the pulse of one's own heartbeat, conveying appreciation, cultivating thought forms of beauty and health within one's mind—powerful fertilizer of a different kind is released.

Trees are so often taken for granted, and used without much thought, for the benefit of the human species. Samsara, the Hindu and Buddhist term for the cycle of life of all living beings (birth, death, rebirth), is sometimes interpreted as "suffering." In many ways, trees do suffer at the hands of humans. I interpret the concept of suffering as "learning" the sometimes painful lessons necessary for moving ahead on a personal spiritual path. Thought of by some as karma, suffering is remediated or mitigated by freely and willingly giving service to benefit other living beings, and by cultivating a reverence for all life.

We can make more forest-garden places like this one, especially in tiny city and town and backyard spaces, to bring health to the planet, and to ourselves. A solution for the Earth resides in the trees whose transpiration brings more oxygenation and rain to the planet. Without trees, the planet slowly turns to desert. This is not a myth, it is a fact. "It breaks my heart when the Earth is suffering. Trees have always been my fallback," says Eric softly, looking up from where we sit in the middle of the new forest.

WINTER THOUGHTS

Chapter Seventeen

WINTER THOUGHTS

I AM LISTENING TO THE Brahms Trio No. 1 in B major, Op.8, bringing memories from childhood of stealing out of bed, and hiding on the top step of the landing upstairs, when I am supposed to be in bed. Brahms is my mother's favorite composer. She is playing cello brilliantly and passionately, along with my piano teacher Isidore Freeman and Ken Dean, a big Irishman who holds his small priceless Strad fearlessly in his big hands. My father dozes in his chair while Ken's wife is in the kitchen cleaning up after dinner. It is the shortest day of the year, just before Christmas, and one of my finest memories of happy times in my family.

Many years have passed since that Trio. It's the Solstice, again, and people have invited me over but I don't feel like getting dressed up and going out. I just want to celebrate the quiet of this favorite evening alone. Celebrations will come at better times. I burn some sage and cedar, and turn in early. Down comforters and books are my friends tonight.

My favorite season is winter. Despite this, a kind of sadness envelops me, as I am aware of the winding down of the slow, languid days of summer, and the hopeful autumn gathering of stores in for winter. This is a time for contemplation and introspection, for comprehension of what has passed, of deepening wisdom and of integration. Solstice signals the end of the long days and ahead are months of sub-zero, ice-bound early mornings. Now, coming into winter, the cold, crisp wisdom days are ahead.

This is my season. I seem to know it best, as if I have spent season upon season of many lifetimes here. Inside, I am grateful for shelter and warmth, as the elements beat hard against the walls of my Colorado cabin. I know the tall Pines are bending, impossibly bending, then yielding. It is too late to go out into the forest, though it calls.

Red, my old dog, is my only companion this evening. He's not well, and I give him tasty organic, gluten free treats that I bake especially for him made from flax seed, peanut butter, pumpkin, and brown rice flour. They are so good that I eat some of the broken ones while waiting for them to cool. Now, he is sleeping by my bed on this special night. I kiss him goodnight on his third eye in the middle of his forehead. His gift to me is his loving devotion. Gazing directly into my eyes, he tells me he is happy by thumping his tail. He waits until he thinks I am asleep, then he gets up and very quietly creeps back to his dog bed. He watches out for me.

Winter Thoughts

The house is empty, my partner has moved out. I am comfortable in my reclaimed space, I've been here before, yet it is lonely. Now, when the wind howls and the fire in the wood stove gets low, I'm the only one here who can get up and do something about it. I pull the blanket up around my head. Eventually, I go back to sleep.

In the morning, to find connection, I get bundled up and, leaving the dog whose bad hips keep him home, go out back into the Comanche Peaks Wilderness, up the mountain, to visit my friends, the Ponderosas. Walking the forest leaves my prints, where at other times I pass unnoticed except by the trees. Silence weighs upon a branch, white and slow. The quiet awareness of trees is ever present, magnificent.

Snow is getting deep. I unclip snowshoes from my pack and keep going, sucking air in searing breaths, glasses fogging, heart beating hard. Towering trees overhead unpredictably dump piles of snow off branches, and onto me, when it becomes too much for them. The stark outlines of the Spruces are striking against bright white. There is a deep peace in this winter forest, as a halo of sun lights the way through the trees. Tracking the bobcat in my snowshoes hoping for a glimpse, I never see her, just her furry tracks. I dust a foot of snow off a log, sit, and look out over the expanse of wilderness, Long's Peak in the distance.

I want it to be magnificent, but it just doesn't feel the way I hoped. I was looking for something, not sure what, on this first day of winter. Undaunted, I make meaning of the day—write a poem, take a few snapshots, collect juniper berries and pine cones. The clouds roil fearfully, as though there will be an afternoon storm, and suddenly scurry back toward the horizon. Then, snow falls. Silence drifts down over everything, and I feel a deep stillness.

Eventually, I get cold. I place a crystal at the base of a tree, say a blessing and hurry back. Past the old Cedar and the patch of pointed Juniper, and the familiar split Pine. Down the crystal mountain. Past the fire pit that my partner artfully constructed and we never used because of risk of wildfires, and the meditation circle. Past the gardens, beds covered for the season, through the gates. And moving fast now, back to a warm house and a cup of tea.

The day after Solstice feels full, though by conventional standards, I haven't done anything. Nothing lacking, everything so simple and satisfying. I made connection with the land, and communed with the spirits of the trees. Today, the bobcat walked nonchalantly across the deck. I saw her through the window. For one moment, she turned her head and looked at me. She chose her time.

COMMUNION

Chapter Eighteen

COMMUNION

IN THE HEART OF THE Roosevelt National Forest near Estes Park, Colorado, I am building a memorial of branches and stones on a rock outcropping, for my mother, in commemoration of the ten years since her passing. She loved the mountains in this part of the country, near where she lived. A large Ponderosa Pine, branches overhanging, as if embracing the shrine, begins to talk to me.

He says, conversationally, "I am in the woods. I have seen many things pass. I watch. This rock and I are together." I place my hands on him and receive a feeling of peace; on his part, he responds with a sense of gratitude, simply saying, "Touch." His chestnut red, rough scored bark, gleams in the sun. He might be quite old. People also want touch, especially when older. I reflect that trees frequently begin communication by describing their location, commenting upon the other beings around them, and by stating what they have "seen."

Something deep in me shifts whenever I am around Ponderosas. I've been drawn to them ever since I have lived here, and now I know why. I have the conviction that they are my true medicine trees. I feel so comforted by them, and I understand that I can tell them about things I have not done well enough in my life, and make restitution by taking care of them. So, from there on in, I talk with this one, of my relationship with my mother—and of everything.

These Pines are dignified and stalwart. There is much wind here in Colorado, and when it blows, it gusts. The branches give gracefully, and just when about to break, give some more. They stand tall upon rocky hills of rose quartz, red lichen laced granite, and mica glinting in the sun. The ones on top are beautifully stunted by the elements, some with roots reaching literally through rock, steady old sentinels, those who make it.

The Pondies, as I call them affectionately, are friendly trees, and on the alert for communication. The sense I get is that most of them are waiting for the chance to commune with humans, who they like. Once in awhile there is a curmudgeon who is disdainful of my paltry efforts, and indicates that as clearly as if turning away a shoulder. Usually, though, The Ponderosas are pleased and like to talk.

Gradually over the years, I have developed a way of approaching tree communication that all trees seem to respond to pretty well. The first order of importance in communication is respect. Along with this, is the importance of intention for the greatest good, and openness to receive information without judgment or modification. It is no different from any authentic human to human interaction, in that regard.

How does it work? First, I ready myself by clearing energy off my body with a simple breath-work method; the old way used to be a dip in an ice cold stream, or a sage smudge. Then I raise my arms high, hands outstretched to the sky, and invoke Spirit, in the form that comes to me, which in my case, includes Reiki. I give gratitude to my Higher Self and the Creator, to my guides and to the guardians of the Earth, for this day.

Because I am outside in nature, I pray to the directions to establish sacred space: to the East, I honor the place of the rising sun and new life; to the South, the place of the grandmothers and nurturance of the earth; to the West, the place of the dancing bear and enlightenment; to the North, the place of the grandfathers, and wisdom bison.

I place an offering on the ground, to Earth, usually something that calls to me on the path. Today it is a little piece of white quartz. I put it under a baby Ponderosa Pine who I barely miss stepping on, growing right next to my foot. I like this ritual. Lastly, I end with Sky, where I ask the Creator to bless and witness these offerings. That is just one example—how I do it—but people must choose their own personal ways to offer blessings and thanks.

Then I approach the tree, introduce myself, and tell the tree why I am here. If I'm just here, and don't know why, I say, "I am here, my name is Gianna." Then I ask for permission to talk. It is important to note that I am mindfully asking, and that I am genuinely interested in communication as if I were meeting a new person for the first time. If no resistance or objection, I place both hands on the trunk, close my eyes, and wait. Every tree I approach has inner movement that is immediately discernable when I place my hands upon it. To the eye, it is not moving. But, at my third eye, once my hands are there, I feel a circular kind of sensation, almost like a spinning disc, that indicates connection.

At this point, I ask for the tree's name. I have discovered that whatever comes first into my mind is the name. I don't rethink it and I never change it. Interestingly, over the years, it seems that certain species of tree have names that mostly begin with a certain letter. For example, the Pondies seem often to have "M" names. Don't ask me why this is, I have no idea! Trees that are in places where certain names might be linguistically appropriate seem to have all sorts of different names that I have never heard before. So there is no rhyme or reason to it, at least not that I have yet discovered.

After establishing contact, I start a conversation. The most important, and difficult, part of communing with trees is not to manipulate the situation to fit preconceived ideas. So I have developed a few standard questions that seem to work well for trees. Right away, I ask, "What have you seen?" The trees themselves approach conversation this way, and I am just following their lead. My fantasy is that being tall, they can "see" overhead from a different perspective, not only of height, but of time. Or, I ask them what their job is, their mission. Just standing where they are, rooted observers, is a mission they often mention. Also, holding the form for other beings in the forest, is a concept that applies.

I have taken notes for many years, and discover that most of what trees tell me is about the changes that take place around them, because they are rooted in the same place all that time. Afterward, for some of the old ones, I research their information. Had there really been a fire, or train tracks, or fairground nearby? In almost every case, what might be explained away as imagination, turns out to be historical fact. I am blown away by this discovery. And this is one of the things that has given me the courage to write this book!

Thinking about it, I suppose it's possible that trees act as a kind of channel or spirit intermediary between me and some record of time. But not being familiar with channeling myself, and not wanting to be, I think it is possible that trees are able to absorb and store information energetically, impressionistically. This is translated and conveyed to me, once I make contact, almost like a download that starts when I place my hands on them.

I don't think, or talk, I just stay there for several minutes, with my hands touching the tree on the trunk or branch. If I learn something, I report it to the tree. If the tree has expressed concerns or emotions, like the Beech grove at my old house in Maine, I reflect back what I think or feel about what the tree have said. I always try to find something truthful and positive to express that reflects what they have told me. I approach working with trees like I approach being a therapist or a healer.

Always in my pocket are small natural quartz crystals that I collect as I walk, for placing upon a tree that calls to me, or wants healing. I hike all over the mountain, talking with hundreds, taking care of them, using crystal healing. I hold the crystal between my palms and infuse it with energy. I always put a blessing into it, as in the case of an ailing tree, or a manifesting idea that relates to something that has passed between us. I let my intuition tell me what to do and then where to put it on the tree.

At one time, every Pondie in a space of at least 10 acres around my cabin held a crystal in a notch on a branch. The direction is important. I place the crystal intuitively in the direction from which the tree needs the greatest protection. This might be from the weather, or from humans. Or, I bury one at the base of the tree, depending upon what intuition indicates is best.

If I am called by a tree who is not well, I perform a healing ceremony of greater length. I target the issue the tree tells me about more specifically. Sometimes it is an obvious physical issue, like a sapling that has been stripped by elk rutting, a bear scraping his back on the bark, or a bad case of mistletoe that is sucking the life out of a tree. Sometimes it is an emotional issue, like a habitat that is threatened. Or, sometimes a spiritual issue, harder to define, which comes under the category of being out of step with nature. Maybe it is a transplant, or a tree who has no companions of its own, or is nearing the end of its life.

In Colorado, many Evergreens are dying or dead, who were in full health the year before, due to the pine beetle infestation. I am told that the cycle takes about ten years to run its course. I'm sympathetic, but insects are living beings and have their life cycles too. Natural death in nature by fire and flood and earthquake makes space for new growth. There is wisdom behind apparent chaos.

COMMUNION

In the long run, my layperson's perspective is that using chemical solutions is ultimately worse than just letting the bugs do their thing. It's the old story of how much or little to intervene. Not that I wouldn't try to save a tree by putting pheromone packets on the Old Ones. Like the old Doug Fir who shields my cabin from howling wind and blizzard in the winter and cools it in the summer. Everyone urges me to cut him down, but I will not—he's over a century old and in vibrant health. I would rather lose my deck!

Once a tree is compromised, or growing weak for some reason, it is vulnerable to attack, and crowding is supposedly one of the issues. On the Islands off the coast of Maine, the dense Spruce forests succumb every 50 years or so to Spruce budworm. Recently, I sail back to a forested island where I had picnicked under the boughs of a mighty Spruce, to find nothing but brittle, orange skeletons reaching up into the sky. Insects make short work of the trees once they get going. I feel sad.

Yet, the trees tell me differently. When I ask trees who have been attacked by something or someone, sap running down their bodies like water, they tell me things like, "my time has come, I am ready", or, "I have seen many things and I am content." If only humans could take a page from the stoic acceptance of these trees of their fate. Such tree wisdom, and other healing experiences extended from trees to humans, come from the spirit of trees. With their timeless healing gifts, trees have much to offer us. In return, they deserve from humans the kind of care that we show other living beings.

At the end of communing with trees, I offer them a symbol of thanks—a gesture, a word, a prayer—anything from my heart that conveys appreciation for the trees' willingness to communicate with me. This shows respect for the honor of communing with a living being of another species. I may be moved to say a few words, to acknowledge in my own way, the unique human-tree interchange of energy that has taken place. Sometimes the tree does this too.

This is not projection, fantasy or delusion. What I am doing in communing with trees is translating. I'm tapping into a vibrational frequency, a waveform of energy that comes via subtle channels of perception. Such transmission is possible because of the human capacity for intuitive ways of knowing, sensing and perceiving. We have all experienced this in our lives with other human beings, and with animals. It sometimes feels like love.

The more I know about trees, the more I know about living beings. Not only of the animals, insects and the stones that live with them, also of the earth, wind and sky. Trees, just standing where they are rooted, are the sentinels of the forest. They hold the form for a vast ecosystem. Human appreciation for that role is important for them to hear. They are true stewards of the land.

Chapter Title

WATER AND EARTH

Chapter Nineteen

WATER AND EARTH

Years ago, sailing back from Canada along the coast of Downeast Maine, in driving rain, gusting wind pushing the boat faster than hull speed should allow, a crashing sound is heard over the high pitched wail of bare shrouds. The boat is seaworthy and well constructed—I never doubt her. There is no way to know the source of that sound, or whether it is dangerous. In any case, there is nothing to be done about it at the moment, white knuckling it along a lee shore. I'm just so glad, at times like this, not to be alone on board.

Arriving finally at a gunk hole with a tricky entrance, anchored safely in heavy, dark fog, I fall, fully clothed, into sleep. The night is strange with birds seeming to be on board, calling to one another as if an arm's length away, in the unnaturally silent air. It disturbs me enough to awaken, and go on deck for a look around, but I see nothing, as thick fog obscures my own outstretched hand.

The next morning, *Kachina* is nestled inside a deep, tiny pool ringed round with rocks. There is no exit at low tide. Birds, seals, mussels and all manner of scurrying creatures tightly encircle the spirit boat. The bolder among them come to sit on the amas. It takes hours for the tide to come up again. The origin of that sound was never discovered— could have been lightening, or a piece of flying debris. One determined little Pine clings tenaciously to the only rock still visible when motoring out. It causes me to reflect on the life that little Pine and I have in common...

Another time, skiing alone across the frozen lake down the road from my house, I am crossing the very middle, feeling the expanse and freedom of it all, admiring the Evergreens ringing round the sharp silver whiteness, when sharp, loud cracks pierce the silence, one after another. I freeze, and stop breathing. Then I carefully look around, barely moving my head. The Spruce on shore glisten with ice. I look down at my feet for what seems like a long time, controlling the almost inescapable impulse to run for it. I know that ice cracks, as water moves deep beneath, and I also know that this ice is several feet thick. I remember where I am, breathe again, gingerly move one leg, then another.

These kinds of experiences upon water alert me to the feeling of the smallness of my being, the slim thread holding me to life. Nature's immensity is absolute. If nature wishes, whether on ocean or lake, I might be instantly swallowed, never to be found.

What is it about confronting danger? I suppose it's the feeling of having escaped death, being flooded with life. The dangers of normal everyday living: vehicular crashes, pollution, drought, floods, tornados, famine, war, fatal illness, are taken for granted. Perhaps, in order to entertain the fantasy of being in charge, we choose to ignore danger, rather than be at the mercy of what we have no control over. In storms, trees are wild; on calm days, they are tranquil. Sometimes I seek the adrenalin rush of full engagement with the elements, to emphasize a sense of being alive. Sometimes, intensity and heightened awareness can be experienced in a way that slows down, rather than speeds up, the nervous system—as in meditation. In nature, I find both at the same time.

There is an exhilarating, yet peaceful place on a mountain in Maine on Mt. Desert Island, where a particular combination of wind and movement of waves in the ocean below, combines with the grounding of earth and rock above. Cairns form miniature Asian looking archways and molecules seem to visibly dance in the air. Out over the edge of the cliff, the ocean stretches all the way across the Atlantic. Stunted by wind, small Pines survive the harsh freezing winter temperatures. Their vibrations hold the energy for this little circle of stones and trees. This same kind of spiritual feeling occurred for me when touching the ancient stones at Carnac and Stonehenge, and the ancient trees. Stones and trees, humans and trees, there is resonance among all forms of life.

Ten years ago, I left the NorthEast Coast to move West, and SouthWest, seeking openness and simplicity, along the way giving up the things and works and activities of my former life. I always seek out the earth, and trees. Anchored in a cove off an uninhabited island—uninhabited, that is, except by all of life—I go ashore to walk in the mossy, cool understory of tall Spruce, sit upon roots crisscrossed above the ground. It's what I call, 'going to ground.' When I am traveling, or have no secure home, and am suddenly grabbed by that slight feeling of dislocation, I stop at a park or woods, and walk until I can't see anything other than trees, shrubs, bushes, flowers, grass, rocks. I am immediately rebalanced. Earth provides foundation, attachment, security. Simply to touch the earth—to walk, dance, share together in beauty—is to be more alive.

There are similarities between the expanses of water and expanses of land with their unending spaces of apparent nothingness, empty of humans. The eye sees far, goes over horizons, perspective bends back into itself. It's an infinite exploration of the unknown, the Great Mystery. To me, these spaces are full. The Gnostics, Zen masters, and countless other sages talk of the nothingness that encompasses everything. There is really no difference, between water and earth, in this regard.

I miss the water ocean, yet I am always finding a new earth ocean of trees to nourish my soul—in the brilliant New England autumn hardwoods, in the deep forests so full with leaves that the sky is hidden overhead; in the quiet stands of mountain evergreens, needles and cones thick underfoot; in the subtle deserts among red and orange rock; in the wilderness preserves of the world. And especially, in the ancient groves of the Old Ones.

As I move through these varied landscapes and experiences, I am unburdened of the past. However, I sometimes feel as though a part of my soul has been left behind, with so many changes reflecting the ebb and flow of my life. At such times, trees are my teachers. They inform me of what they have seen in their lives, and remind me that change is not only inevitable, but beneficial. In order to survive and thrive, their seasonal cycles are necessary. We are not such different beings—always beginning and growing, moving and integrating, creating and completing.

Walking forward in beauty, surrounded by the restorative energy of nature, the spirit of trees is always with me. Trees are patient and wise beings—models for living in harmony with all my relations, and with myself. We know each other and share the same earth, water and air. Together, we celebrate the continuity of life.

CPSIA information can be obtained
at www.ICGtesting.com
Printed in the USA
FSOW01n2151141017
39873FS

9 781457 554254